SPORTING
ANCESTORS

SPORTING ANCESTORS

TRACING
YOUR
FAMILY'S
ATHLETIC
PAST

KEITH GREGSON

The
History
Press

First published 2012

The History Press
The Mill, Brimscombe Port
Stroud, Gloucestershire, GL5 2QG
www.thehistorypress.co.uk

British Library Cataloguing in Publication Data.
A catalogue record for this book is available from the British Library.

ISBN 978 0 7524 5839 7

Typesetting and origination by The History Press
Printed in the EU for The History Press.

CONTENTS

The author in 1950s Manchester United football kit. (Author's collection)

PREFACE

With the onward march of modern technology it has now become much easier to 'unearth the skeletons' of direct ancestors and their siblings from Victorian times onwards. But skeletons are not enough. We all want to know what these ancestors were like, what they thought and what made them 'tick'. If the nineteenth-century French medieval historian Michelet is right then we really are 'the sum of our ancestors' – and there can be no more rewarding aspect of family history than putting flesh onto ancestral bones.

Should this argument be accepted then a book about the role of sport in ancestral life will be of considerable interest and use to family historians. Most families have some form of connection with sport, usually at amateur level, but some might discover that an ancestor was a local champion runner or cricketer. These ancestors were not necessarily full time or professional but such has been the impact of sport on British life over the last century and a half that it has left an indelible impact. It has also left records and the everlasting popularity of sport means that these records stretch from accounts of mighty cricket test matches to ones relating to the humblest of games on the village green. Press coverage also extends from cup finals at Wembley to local league meetings between the Co-op and Post Office in Barrow-in-Furness on a wet Wednesday afternoon.

Medals, trophies, photographs, newspaper cuttings – many survive to be handed down in families. National, regional and local research centres have relevant archives and many sports clubs have managed to keep hold of archives naming literally hundreds of ordinary folk who have played sport both for profit and for fun.

During a televised broadcast of the 2010 Wimbledon tennis championship, a camera panning the audience came to rest on an older couple. The commentator noted that they were the parents of one of the current players – the mother had been a top swimmer and the father an international canoeist. 'Sport must be in the genes,' the commentator noted. What follows may help to prove this statement to be true.

My birth certificate bears the legend 'Wembley', which is a good start. Sport plays a part in my own family history. I played cricket, football and rugby (badly) in my youth and coached mini rugby and ran a rugby club mini section in the 1990s. I completed the London Marathon on three occasions and the Great North Run on nineteen. I am a season ticket holder at Sunderland AFC and a supporter of hometown Carlisle United. One son (now in his 30s) is a competition-winning golfer. A second son (retired through injury) captained a county rugby side containing members of the current England First XV and coached. A third represented Great Britain at American football, played rugby for Sunderland First XV and is now seriously involved in mixed martial arts.

I have written extensively on the history of sport for some thirty years, starting in the 1970s with an article on the story behind the hunting song 'John Peel' and progressing through a whole range of articles and a BBC local history series on professional boat racing in Victorian times. This interest in boat racing is ongoing, as witnessed by a lead feature on this topic in *Ancestors* magazine in the early twenty-first century. More recently I have written a rugby club history.

In the last few years I have worked closely with the award-winning sports historian Professor Mike Huggins (now retired from the University of Cumbria). We developed an unusual research area in using song as a source for sporting history. This has led to lectures in Aarhus (Denmark), Budapest, Stirling and Leeds, and to numerous joint publications in peer-reviewed journals. In other words, though not much of sportsman myself, I am 'sport mad' and hope that what follows will be of use to others of a similar bent who are interested in researching their family trees.

How to Use this Book

The terms 'Victorian 'and 'Edwardian' appear frequently in the book. These are used strictly as Victorian (1837–1901) and Edwardian (1901–10). The Victorian era has been subdivided. The early Victorian period covers the years from 1837 to the middle of the 1850s, with the mid-Victorian period running from there to 1880 and the late Victorian period then taking us up to 1901. There are also occasional references to the period just after the Napoleonic Wars, which came to an end in 1815. The years from 1910 to 1914 are described as 'just before the First World War'; the war itself covering the years from 1914 to 1918. The inter-war years stretch from 1918 to 1939.

The book concentrates mainly on the discovery of sporting ancestors in the Victorian and Edwardian periods. There are a number of reasons for this. In the first place, these are important periods in the development of British sport as the Industrial Revolution took a grip and the balance of population moved from countryside to town. Though for many living in towns and cities leisure time was at a premium, it was often used for sport and the gregarious nature of town life naturally led to the development of team games and competition. At the same time, these were periods during which the recording of personal and sporting information was on the increase, and ancestors become easier to discover and monitor than they were previously. Although this particular review of ancestral sport is carried on in some cases beyond the First World War, it doesn't go much further into what might be regarded as 'living memory'. In general, living memory may now start at the Second World War or even later but, as explained in the chapter on sources, at least we have the advantage over earlier periods in having first-hand recordings (spoken and visual) from much of the post-First World War period. This was rarely the case for earlier times.

In terms of pure geography, the sporting ancestry covered in this book extends across the British Isles and there are references throughout to areas now in the United Kingdom and the Republic of Ireland. However, there is a leaning towards the English experience, partly because of the relative size of the English population and partly because of the author's own research background and experience. Within England too there is a tendency to use more examples from the north than from other regions despite conscious efforts to find a balance. As these examples can generally be used to aid research carried out elsewhere in the British Isles this 'bias' may be excused. There is also little space to deal with the British abroad, i.e. those playing or spreading sport beyond our shores.

A conscious decision has also been made to divide ancestral sporting experience into two categories: amateur and professional. This does not always work. Sometimes it is difficult to prove that those who played 'for amusement alone' were not benefiting financially from their involvement in sport. This benefit could range from a few pennies in a boot for transport coverage to a complete professional 'shamateurism'. In cricket in particular it was claimed that the cunning amateur, wealthy as he might be, could make more out of the game from 'perks' than the relatively impoverished professional. All this noted, the headings are convenient and generally work – and where they don't every effort has been made to point this out.

Finally, as far as these notes are concerned, a warning as to the problems that have to be faced when dealing with the simple word 'sport'. Today we may have our own picture of what constitutes sport, or a sport, but that picture may not be the same as the one envisaged in the past. This problem can be observed in a wonderful statement made by William Grenfell (1855–1945) in the 1930s. Also known by his title, Lord Desborough, he is a fine example of one type of English sportsman of his time. He rowed for Oxford in the boat race, won medals for fencing and was a top administrator in cricket, tennis, fencing and rowing. His use of the words 'sport', 'games' and 'pastimes' are particularly intriguing, though possibly confusing:

> The old order changeth, yielding place to the new, and perhaps during the last fifty years more changes have taken place in sport than in most activities. But how is sport to be defined? Does it include games such as cricket, football,

rowing, athletics, polo, and lawn tennis? Or should it be confined to hunting, shooting, fishing, stalking, coursing, and other pastimes perhaps more strictly sporting? Sport would seem to imply the pursuit of some quarry, even if it were only rats, and if there is a spice of danger attending it, so much the better.

From an essay 'Sport of Many Kinds' in *Fifty Years Memories and Contrasts: A Composite Picture of the Period 1882–1932* (*The Times*, London, 1932) p. 196.

British Sporting History: an Introduction

Before Victoria (up to 1837)

The problem with studying sport and sporting ancestors in Britain prior to the early nineteenth century is not so much a lack of sporting activity as a lack of records. Evidence suggests that human beings have indulged in sport since the dawn of time. While Britain remained rural and communities isolated, little was noted down on the sporting front and even less on the success of individuals. A recent survey of village life in rural North Cumberland in the eighteenth century came to the conclusion that songs of the day were perhaps the best evidence for sporting activity – and activity there was in the shape of horse racing, wrestling, running, jumping and throwing.

Despite these drawbacks, it is still possible to discover something about those who succeeded at a higher level in the popular sports of the day. This is particularly true from the time of the Civil War and the Restoration of Charles II in the late seventeenth century. Charles was not only 'merry' but also sports mad, and took an active interest in a wide range of sporting activities.

By the time sport took off as a truly popular activity in Victorian times, a variety of ball-kicking sports had been around for centuries. Football, or foot-ball as it was commonly known, seems to have been popular since the first victorious warrior decided to kick the severed head of a defeated foe around the battlefield. There is also a written record of football activity in Scotland during the Middle Ages.

The starting point for Orkney ball game. (Author's collection)

The best known and longest lasting form of foot-ball is that associated with annual Shrovetide or Pancake Day celebrations. Places such as Alnwick in Northumberland, Workington on the Cumbrian Coast and Kirkwall, capital of the Orkney Islands, share a similar heritage in such a game. In the case of Orkney a plaque outside its Cathedral of St Magnus gives a brief synopsis of the game and its origins. These games usually took place between residents of different areas of the town or village and often became so anarchic that in some places they were eventually banned. There were virtually no rules and serious injury was common. Shops were closed and boarded up for the day, while pubs did a roaring trade. The annual match at Alnwick has survived mainly because organisers moved the pitch from the centre of the town to meadows on the outskirts. Today both residents and keen visitors take part and the contest remains spirited. Goals, or hales as they were sometimes called, were a rarity with the scorer rewarded and his name often recorded for posterity.

Shrovetide foot-ball was not the only form of this sport played in earlier times. There is evidence of activity in that birthplace of many a great foot-baller: the schoolyard. Eighteenth-century Anglo-Scottish poet Susanna Blamire has left us this delightful account of a kick around in a village schoolyard in the middle of that century:

For races some, but more for football cry
Mark out their ground and toss the globe on high;
The well-fought field deals many a galling stroke
And many a chief's o'erthrown, and many a shin is broke

Our modern forms of the game also developed from versions played at public schools such as Eton, Rugby and Harrow. What rules there were differed slightly from school to school, but they shared with the Shrovetide form of the game a hero worship of the goal scorer and a tendency towards 'mob violence'. Though organised by the boys themselves, the games were encouraged by the staff and were seen as a way of improving both school morale and morals – both of which were in decline in the early nineteenth century. Some records of these games have survived.

One early ancestor worth having would be William Webb Ellis, who is credited with picking up the ball and running with it and creating forever a link between his school, Rugby, and the popular sport of today. Rugby Union's World Cup carries his name despite a number of modern sports historians disputing his stature as the single 'inventor' of the modern game.

The story of the beginnings of organised cricket is one of gradual development between the Civil War of the seventeenth century and the days of Queen Victoria. There is evidence for cricket being played in the reign of Charles II, culminating in the first recorded 'county match' between London County and Kent, which took place in 1719. This took place on Lamb's Conduit Fields in London, later to gain a reputation as a dumping ground for the capital's sewerage.

The laws of cricket began to take shape in the eighteenth century with 1774 and 1788 both key dates. They were then revised in 1835. Set against these major developments were others of importance. The first Lord's Cricket Ground and the Marylebone Cricket Club (MCC) date back to 1787. The initial Eton and Harrow cricket match took place in 1805, with gentlemen and players first coming together the following year. Oxford met Cambridge for the first time in 1827, and the first of the modern counties, Sussex, traces its cricketing roots back to 1836.

Horse racing has existed in one form or another ever since man has used horses and ridden on horseback. Here Roman chariot racing springs most readily to mind, as well as the mad dashes that took place in Britain when the wealthier classes were out hunting. As with cricket, the Restoration period was an important one for the development of horse racing and

Chester Racecourse, still in operation today, was in use from an even earlier date. Both Royal Ascot and Epsom have been on the go since the early eighteenth century and The Derby was first run in 1780. The Carlisle Bell remains one of Britain's oldest horse races.

Tennis also existed in many places and in many forms although, unlike Wimbledon (until relatively recently at least), it was an indoor game and differed from the much later 'lawn' tennis. Real tennis and rackets were two forms of the game with a courtly tennis enjoying particular favour in pre-revolutionary France. Tennis was as much the 'sport of kings' as horse racing. Rackets/racquets was very much an indoor game – and had to be for, as one historian has noted, it was played chiefly in taverns and debtors' prisons during the early nineteenth century.

Pedestrianism (at this time defined almost entirely as walking at pace round a selected track) enjoyed immense popularity in the early nineteenth century too, especially in the years immediately following the Napoleonic Wars. Competitions were frequently one-on-one or simply based upon time and distance with heavy betting and backing involved. The Napoleonic Wars also saw the beginning of an important military involvement in sport, with wider athletics meetings traceable back to Sandhurst Academy in 1810.

During the same period prizefighting, or pugilism, also enjoyed an enormous popularity, mainly because it too involved heavy betting and backing. Although the sport flirted with the law and was a moveable feast, those who worked *within* the law were among its most fervent supporters. Up until the 1830s fights were carried out mainly under rules devised by John Broughton, who has been awarded the title 'the Father of the English School of Boxing'.

Although boat racing, or aquatics, was later to enjoy a professional status equal to prizefighting, many of the sport's early participants took part simply for pleasure. The first boat race between Oxford and Cambridge Universities took place in 1829 with the Wingfield Sculls contested soon after. On water, and almost universally open water, yachting gained in popularity and once again it was Charles II, the merry monarch, who had a hand in promoting the sport. A keen yachtsman, he was willing to race both family and friends for considerable sums of money.

The later Stuart period saw a spell of extremely cold weather that increased the incidence of skating as both a sport and a pastime. For months on end the Thames was frozen over with ice thick enough to accommodate contemporary wheeled vehicles. A skating club was also set up in Edinburgh

Charles II, not just 'merry' but sporty too – Taylor, Rev. J., *The Family History of England, Vol. V, 1890–1910* (London). (Author's collection)

in the middle of the eighteenth century. Bowling is another sport with something of a legendary past. Sir Francis Drake famously finished a game on Plymouth Hoe before taking on the Spanish Armada in 1588. A form of this sport also began to enjoy currency in the emerging pit communities of north-east England with betting and backing involved.

There were also sports we recognise today more for their cruelty than their sporting nature – namely bear, bull and badger baiting, and dog and cock fighting. Although for obvious reasons little space will be given to these sports in this book, there is every chance that, in the case of the third of these three sports in particular, ancestral references may turn up in the usual genealogical sources. Cockers and their adherents could be men of standing and wealth in their communities, and have often been written about. The same goes for fox hunting and huntsmen, such as the legendary John Peel who belonged to a large family and has many modern Cumbrians claiming direct descent or a distant relationship (among them the author's own nephew).

To some extent the division between amateur and professional was not a serious issue during these periods. In nearly every major sport fun and gambling were the order of the day, though this was soon to change.

THE REIGN OF QUEEN VICTORIA (1837–1901)

The reign of Queen Victoria was one of the most significant in British social history and in British sporting history, too. It started with Britain a primarily as rural society and ended with it as an urban one suited to the rapid spread of organised sport. Running alongside developments in the recording of data, such as those required for civil registration and decennial censuses, advances in education and newspaper communication made possible the noting down of details relating to much of this sporting activity.

Foot-ball is a classic game in point. In 1837 there were the Shrovetide games, various school matches and occasional kick arounds. By 1901 association football (soccer), Rugby Union and Rugby League were all structured and recognised sports played and supported by many. Association football ('the dribbling game') has become such a part of the British way of life that it is now recognised by the word football alone. It developed steadily as a sport throughout the Victorian period with a particular surge in the 1870s and '80s. Rules were codified at Cambridge University in 1848 and the first recognisable club was set up in Sheffield nine years later. The oldest of the league clubs, Notts County, dates from 1862.

In terms of structure, 1863 was a special date for football with the formation of the English Football Association (FA). Its cup was first played for in the 1871/2 season with internationals starting around the same time.

A league structure took longer and had to await the formation of the English Football League in 1888. Recent research indicates that there was a real upsurge of local football during the years between the founding of the FA and the Football League, with teams playing friendlies and entering cups – often organised at county level. The public schools were also heavily involved, helping to establish the laws of the game and setting up old boys' clubs.

The formation of the Football League was a highly significant development with the twelve initial teams (all still playing today) divided between Lancashire and the Midlands. It was also during the Victorian period that football lay down its roots in other parts of Britain. Scotland's oldest club, Queen's Park, was formed in 1867 with the Scottish FA and its cup first played just under a decade later. The initial international between England and Scotland took place in 1872, with the Scottish side made up entirely of Queen's Park players. The Scottish League was set up in 1891. The links between English and Welsh football has always been strong at league club and cup level. Wrexham was formed in the early 1870s, Cardiff and Swansea later in the century. The Welsh FA was set up in 1878. Ireland's oldest football club is Cliftonians, formed in 1879. The Irish FA and its cup were set up in 1880 and the league dates back to 1890.

What is now known as Rugby Union gathered in strength in the 1870s and, in many areas, kept its head in front of football (association) and was still known simply as 'football' in many local newspapers. Between 1870 and the middle of the 1880s, the home internationals' calendar was set up. Oxford began its games with Cambridge in the 1871/2 season and the influential Hospitals Cup had its first winner in Guys in 1875. The 1870s and '80s also saw the commencement of both county and inter-county cups. Yorkshire dominated the early county championships in the 1890s. By this time, many major rugby clubs had been established.

The major rift in rugby, 'the carrying game' (examined more carefully in The Professionals chapter), came in the middle of the 1890s with the setting up of the Rugby League. The cause of the split was the payment of financial compensation for 'broken time' and the subsequent dispute accented the difference between those who could afford the time to play the sport and those who could not. The breakaway clubs were initially known as the Northern Union and came from Yorkshire and the north-west of England. At first the schism was simply financial and it was only with time that the laws of league changed to make it a recognisably different game from union today. Researchers may be interested to note that Rugby Union clubs carrying the RFC affix were usually founded before the split; those with RUFC came after. League clubs changed their affix from RFC to RLFC after the split (or took up RLFC if a later foundation).

Cricket was more developed than foot-ball when Victoria came to the throne. Like the games of the round and the oval ball, its organisation was recognisably modern by the end of the nineteenth century. By then a first class and minor county structure was in place, and both local league and village cricket had become a part of the British way of life. In all this, the year 1864 and the initial publication of *Wisden*, the famed recorder of all first-class cricketing activity, is key. Yet for the sporting family historian there may be much of interest to be discovered in examining the deeds of the non-first-class teams of wandering professionals set up in the mid-Victorian period to play 'against the odds' (as in a professional XI versus a local XXII). The local team was usually made up of those with talent plus a couple of professional 'ringers'.

The first recognised English cricketing tour was to Canada in 1859; the rivalry with Australia being established across the 1861/2 season. The first test match between the two countries took place in Melbourne in 1877. Nine counties played in what has since been recognised as the first county championship in 1873 – a championship which included all but three of the modern first-class counties by 1900. The Minor Counties Championship got under way in 1895.

Tennis was another sport that really established its modern structure in the Victorian period and also proved an activity enjoyed by both males and females. Among the main features were the move from indoor to outdoor, the commencement of grass or lawn tennis and the initiation of 'Wimbledon'. As trivia experts will be aware, the invention of lawn tennis is laid at the door of Major Walter Clopton Wingfield, who created a game known as sphairistike. Basically a country house pursuit, the game was quickly discarded (or remodelled) and the late 1870s and early '80s saw the development of modern lawn tennis. Both cricket and croquet took an early interest but cricket, in the shape of the MCC, soon backed out, leaving tennis to be organised by the All England Croquet and Tennis Club. The Wimbledon men's singles championship dates back to 1877 and the women's to 1884. The Lawn Tennis Association (LTA) was founded in 1888.

Another racquet sport, squash, generally associated with the twentieth century, also has nineteenth-century origins. During the 1870s the boys of Harrow School used a soft ball in their warm-up procedure for hard

An early croquet lady in *Punch*. (Author's collection)

ball racquets and gradually this caught on. Competitive badminton just shaded into the nineteenth century with the commencement of the All England Championships in 1899. Badminton had already been a pastime for a number of years and was popular with females.

In terms of athletics, the pre-Victorian period is best known for the development of professional pedestrianism, though there is evidence for a wider interest in military circles and 'leaping' and 'throwing' in village sports. With the Victorian period, general interest eventually moved from walking to running and amateur athletics took root in the universities (Cambridge in 1857 and Oxford in 1860). The Amateur Athletics Association (AAA) was formed in 1880 with its first championships being for men alone. Early events included the 100, 440 and 880yds, and the 1 mile and 10 mile race. Hurdles were over a distance of 120yds and field events included the long jump, high jump and pole vault, plus putting the weight and throwing the hammer.

At a local level, football, rugby and cricket clubs began to organise bank holiday sports and these attracted large crowds. In many cases the same sports clubs developed fitness clubs as well. Cross-country also came into being as an offshoot from another sport, with the Thames Rowing Club promoting it during the winter months in order to keep its rowers in shape. The first English cross-country championships took place at Roehampton in 1877. Professional athletics moved from the walking track to the running track, taking its audience, betters and backers with it. At tracks across the nation, handicap and scratch races took place across a number of distances – not all of them the same as those raced over by amateurs.

Cycling was a sport that went hand in hand with athletics and grass cycle racing was a common sight at Victorian athletic events. Cycling itself is acknowledged as a very Victorian pastime and up until the late 1880s competition was carried out on penny-farthings and tricycles. By 1889 safety bicycles were replacing these in competitions. Events also began to take place over considerable distances including London to Brighton and Lands End to John O'Groats.

Most of the sports in the athletic spectrum were eventually to benefit from the foundation of the modern Olympics at the very end of the Victorian era; the result of Frenchman de Coubertin's love of English amateurism and his experience at the 'Much Wenlock Olympics'. The modern Olympics were held in Athens in 1896 and Paris in 1900. Many Britons became involved. One modern Olympic sport from the outset was weightlifting, which started to enjoy currency around the time the Olympic movement was revived. The first Open Championship was held in London in 1891 and there were successful weightlifting Britons at the first Modern Olympics in Athens five years later.

The reign of Victoria was a great period for both amateur and professional boat racing. By 1861 the Wingfield Sculls, amateur singles championship of the Thames, was firmly established. In the same decade Oxford University was totally dominant in the annual boat race. Amateur championships involving pairs, fours and eights were also in place by the late Victorian period, alongside the wide-reaching blue riband of single sculling, the Diamond Challenge Sculls.

Between 1840 and 1880 professional boat racing was one of the nation's leading sports. As with prizefighting, running and wrestling, betting and backing were mainly responsible for this. Naturally, the sport enjoyed its largest popularity near to the rivers and enclosed waters where the rowing was carried out. There was a great rivalry between the Thames and the Tyne, with the Clyde also a rowing river of importance. Professional aquatics were to be seen on Loch Lomond and the tiny Talkin Tarn near Brampton in Cumberland as well. The sport was practised in single sculls, pairs, fours and eights, though generally the single sculls attracted the most attention. It continued well into the twentieth century, however the rise of association football in particular meant that the great days of the sport came to an end in the early 1880s. Yachting, firmly established on open waters thanks to the enthusiasm of Charles II, began to move 'inland'. In 1860 the Windermere Yacht Club was set up in the English Lake District and the Yacht Racing Association came into being fifteen years later.

One of horse racing's most prestigious events dates back to the very year of Victoria's accession. The first Grand National was run in the mid-1830s at Maghull near Liverpool before moving to its current venue at Aintree. Although horse racing was firmly established as a popular sport by then, it wasn't until a few years later that a jockeys' championship was established for flat racing, with a championship for owners and trainers coming into effect towards the end of the reign. The National Hunt Jockeys Championship first appeared in the year before Victoria's death but by then horse racing was well established. Research has shown that it drew interest from all classes, despite struggling with an anti-betting lobby for most of the nineteenth century.

The same could be said of prizefighting, although the nineteenth century did see the sport move gradually towards a more acceptable form as boxing. The size of the ring and the legality of certain blows were eventually sorted out, and the roles of umpires, referees and seconds all clarified. From the 1830s to the '60s most prizefighting was carried out under the London Prize Ring Rules, which replaced those operational at an earlier date. Under the Marquis of Queensberry Rules, which succeeded these, the sport gradually moved towards acceptability. The first heavyweight title fight fought wearing gloves took place in 1892, with the names of British heavyweight champions recorded from a slightly earlier date.

Competitive swimming also established itself as a sport during the mid- to late Victorian period. The Metropolitan Swimming Association was formed in 1869, followed five years later by the Swimming Association of Great Britain. The first national championships were held in 1878 and the Amateur Swimming Association (ASA) was operating in one form or another from the mid-Victorian period onwards. Recognisable swimming competitions could be viewed in England and Scotland in the 1870s and '80s, and swimming was included in the modern Olympics from the very start. Games of water polo were also being organised and played during the same period.

Golf is yet another sport with strong links back to Victorian times and to Scotland in particular. Golf professionals began to play for an open championship belt in 1860 and a cup replaced this in 1872. The first amateur championship was held at Hoylake in 1885.

In many ways, the development of field hockey runs alongside that of football. The laws of the game were set up in the 1860s and the Hockey Association formed in 1886, a couple of years prior to the foundation of the Football League. As with swimming and tennis, ladies were involved in the sport from its early days and international matches for both were played in the late Victorian period. The laws of the game were further developed in the 1890s, which also saw the growth of regional hockey. Games between the regions were long an important aspect of hockey and a gateway to international honours. The earliest of these was north versus south played in 1890.

With the development of the empire, the role of the army became increasingly important and, as noted earlier, competitive sport encouraged fitness among other things. The regular army turned to polo in India and brought it back to England as well. Competitions, participated in from the mid-century, were often inter-regimental and not always won by the cavalry regiments. War also interfered with sport, such as the competitions cancelled in the 1870s due to the Afghan Wars. Competitive rifle shooting has a military background too, and was closely linked to the volunteer movement of the 1850s and '60s, which sprang up due to fears as to the intentions of Napoleon Bonaparte's nephew, Napoleon III. Here competition was seen as a way of honing skill rather than improving fitness and rifle shooting was carried out on Wimbledon Common for most of the late Victorian period. This eventually led to the well-known shooting competitions based around Bisley Camp and also to the formation of the National Rifle Association.

One sport which shows how economic, social and sporting history can be closely linked is ice-skating. School textbooks note how eating habits came to change in Britain in the mid-Victorian period thanks to the introduction of refrigeration. This allowed the import of frozen meat from Australasia and the Americas. It also enabled the construction of artificial ice rinks. As a result, the National Skating Association was established in 1879.

The late Victorian period was one where sports associated with British nations beyond England began to organise themselves. Curling, a Scottish sport in the eyes of many, is thought to have originated in the Netherlands. The Grand Caledonian Curling Club was formed in Scotland the year after Victoria came to the throne and went from strength to strength as it gained royal support and patronage. That said, there was little in the way of winter sport in the early Victorian period – with the exception of curling and perhaps developing steeple chasing.

In Ireland the year 1884 saw the formation of the highly influential Gaelic Athletic Association, which was the umbrella organisation for both hurling and Gaelic football. The organisation of these sports has remained consistent with the parish, county and provincial government structure as a basis for play and progress. As a modern Irish historian notes, the association was set up to 'resist the spread of British sports across Ireland'.

Another development was female involvement in sports, which increased considerably over the 1800s. Initially hunting, sailing, archery and croquet were the main ones, but by the end of the century tennis, golf and hockey were also proving attractive. Most of the women participating were from the leisured classes however, and there was little in the way of time, facilities or social practice for females who worked.

The late Victorian period witnessed the growth of the sporting 'club' for cyclists, tennis and rugby players, athletes and footballers. The vast majority of these clubs were peopled by amateurs and gentlemen on the look out for what Mike Huggins calls 'the individual or communal pleasure of play'.

The talk was of fair play and muscular Christianity, yet they were gradually starting to recognise the existence of wage-earning professionalism. In a strangely 'English' way sport managed to acknowledge class divisions while bringing the classes together.

THE TWENTIETH CENTURY

As noted in the introduction, the subject of sporting ancestry is enormous and some boundaries have to be placed on a book of readable length. In consequence, the focus of the book is the Victorian period to the Second World War. In general, the twentieth century saw further development in nearly all of the major sports that had sprung up in Victorian times and before. In most cases progress was broken up by the two major wars of the century, but there was also significant advancement in the field of female involvement in sporting life. However, while International Amateur Athletics Association was founded in 1913, the Women's Amateur Athletics Association had to wait until 1930.

In cricket, Glamorgan and Northants became first-class counties and eventually, in 1992, Durham too. Boxing continued to gain acceptance as it featured as an Olympic sport from Edwardian times onwards. Cross-country internationals started in 1903 and the number of track and field events held at the annual AAA Championships grew steadily.

As to sports new to the twentieth century, the development of motor-ised transport has a great deal to answer for and it was inevitable that both the motor car and the motor bicycle should become sporting vehicles. Surprisingly, perhaps, British involvement in the most famous motorised sport, the Grand Prix, came late and real popularity had to await the second half of the century and Stirling Moss. Motorcycle racing developed at a much earlier date. Time trials are known to have taken place early in the century and the TT races in the Isle of Man date back to 1907. Speedway made its way across to Britain from Australia in the 1920s but, like motor car racing, motocross was essentially a post-war phenomenon.

Despite 'motorisation', horse-driven sport still flourished. Polo, mainly associated with Roehampton, Ranelagh and Hurlingham, had fifteen grounds within a 10 mile radius of Charing Cross by 1914. Show jumping, however, developed much later in the century.

Racquet sports also went off in new directions. Table tennis, a fun game rather than a sport in Victorian times, struggled as ping pong in the Edwardian period and did not really settle as an organised sport until the 1920s. Similarly, squash had to await the formation of the Squash Rackets Association in 1929 for true recognition and it was the second half of the century before there was an explosion of real interest.

Snooker and amateur wrestling were also essentially twentieth-century sports. Considering the popularity of professional wrestling the latter development may come as a surprise, yet it was not until 1904 that the National Wrestling Association (later the British Amateur Wrestling Association) was formed.

Perhaps the sporting twentieth century is best summed up by reference to developments in the Olympic arena. After Paris in 1900, the show moved to the United States where, for reasons of time and transport, European interest was marginal. In 1908, a stroke of bad luck for the Italians brought the Olympics to London with major involvement in many sports for competitors from all over the British Isles. This might prove fertile ground for the family historian. At the same time it would be wise not to get too excited over the relative importance of these early Olympics. Despite further developments at Helsinki in 1912 and legendary Olympics held in Paris (1924) and Berlin (1936), it wasn't until Rome (1960) and television that the Olympics became the global brand it is today. This, on reflection, gives the early modern Olympians a status today they would not have enjoyed in their own lifetimes.

Indeed, this observation may be applied to other major modern sports as well. One early Wimbledon ladies singles champion returned home flushed with success only for her brother to enquire what she had 'been up to today'!

THE PROFESSIONALS

The academic study of the history of sport is a relatively new discipline and tutors and students alike are still struggling with definitions of many key words and concepts. The terms 'professional' and 'amateur' prove particularly challenging. In its widest definition, professional can relate to anyone making any financial gain as a result of playing sport, in its narrowest it could apply only to someone making a full-time living out of sport as a player or coach or, in some cases, as both. In what follows the broader definition has been used with occasional acknowledgements when the line between the professional and the amateur who plays purely for pleasure is a thin one.

ASSOCIATION FOOTBALL

It was only in the late twentieth century that the professional footballer achieved the superstar status associated with him today. George Best, Manchester United and Northern Ireland superstar, was put on a pedestal alongside The Beatles in the late 1960s. Some twenty years earlier, a key member of Portsmouth's successful cup-winning side was wont to dubbin his own boots and to carry them to the ground wrapped in brown paper in the basket of his bicycle.

The history of professionalism in football is not an easy one to follow. The legality of being paid to play the game was not recognised by the Football

Association until the 1880s, and it is worthy of recall that football as we know it had then been in existence since 1863. Without doubt, some of the players were already receiving money and there was much talk about boot money and shamateurism. This was especially true in connection with clubs from northern England and the Scottish players they were introducing into their sides. By the early 1880s there was already a general recognition that it was in order to pay expenses and to cover loss of earnings.

Despite shady dealings in the industrial north there was, according to one modern sport historian, 'no professionalism south of Birmingham before 1888'. This seems to have been the case. Certainly the formation of the football leagues in England in 1888 and Scotland in 1890 are seen as defining moments in the history of professional football, and when England played Scotland in 1896 the England side was made up of five professionals and six amateurs. Professional clubs represented at that time included West Bromwich Albion, Aston Villa, Sheffield Wednesday, Sheffield United and Derby County. When names of players appeared in lists the professionals were acknowledged by their surname alone, as they were in cricket.

By the end of the Edwardian period there were thousands of professional footballers playing in England, including part-timers with other jobs that trained a couple of times a week and turned out on Saturdays. The number continued to increase after the First World War, though some, like school-teachers and those of private means, continued as part-timers or amateurs. In Scotland, the vast majority of professional footballers were part time with the top clubs alone able to fund full-time professionals.

Most of the professional footballers came from the working class – and remained part of it, living in their community and taking part in com-munity activities. In general their pay more than equalled that of skilled workers, and footballers were considered as being much better off than the average unskilled worker. Eventually some were placed in club houses, but that came at a later date. Training was not the same as in the modern game, with much of the day spent playing snooker or billiards, and fitness levels were accordingly lower. Cigarettes, bottles of beer and tots of whisky at half time were not considered as being out of order.

The professional footballer's status was reflected in his pay. At the end of Victoria's reign there was a ceiling of £4 a week. During the inter-war years it stood at £8 a week during the playing season and £6 a week during the close season. International footballers received only £10 per game as late as the 1950s. Soon after this, legal challenges came to the concept of a maximum wage. Victory to the footballers opened the floodgates, leading to what some regard today as crazy money.

The hopes of finding records for regular professional footballing ancestors are high – especially after the formation of the English and Scottish football leagues, a professional association and eventually, in 1907, the current PFA. A couple of examples of research already carried out back this up.

June Chatterton from Sheffield told the story of her footballing grandfather Charlie Lemons in an article in *Family History Monthly* (Christmas 2004). He played amateur football in the Sheffield area before signing professionally for Scunthorpe and Lindsey United in 1919. She was able to establish from records that he was a centre forward and scored a respectable thirty-one goals for the club in two seasons, before moving on to Lincoln City in the third division (North) of the Football League. In his single season there he managed only four goals in twenty-two games. He then transferred to York City for a season. As inside left, he made forty appearances and scored five goals. His name appears on a number of occasions in the history of Scunthorpe FC and June has a photograph of the York City side with all the players named.

Alison Naisby also wrote about her north-east-born Great Uncle Tom in an earlier edition of the same magazine (October 2004). A goalkeeper, he made many appearances for Leeds City between 1907 and 1909. He also appeared for Luton Town and a number of sides in north-east England over a career stretching from 1898 to 1913. He made violins while in Leeds and Alison has photographs of him as footballer and a violinmaker. He served in the First World War, then tried a spot of emigration to the United States, but ultimately returned home and died in 1927. His career record is to be found in Michael Joyce's invaluable book of players' records and in the histories of the relevant clubs.

Information on successful Victorian footballers is relatively easy to find, as seen from the example of the victorious Aston Villa side of the 1890s. Charlie Athersmith (1872–1910) was one of the great characters in this team. He played in five league-winning sides and appeared in three cup finals. On one occasion he borrowed an umbrella from a spectator and scored a goal while using it to keep off the rain. John Devey was a prolific goal scorer for the same team. A Birmingham man, he was accomplished at cricket and played the sport for Warwickshire. He was also a keen member of the Association Footballers' Union, He came from a family of silversmiths and learned the trade himself as a teenager – as witnessed by his entry in the 1881 census.

Much has happened in football since the 1890s and a number of past English league sides, such as Barrow and Workington, now play outside the four major leagues. Some clubs have fallen by the wayside completely, so if an ancestor played for a club professionally and it is no longer in existence, it is still worth checking out. It may well have been a significant league side in the past. Local leagues using semi-professionals developed alongside those leagues (discussed later in The Amateurs chapter), and indeed many of the old amateur teams of the mid-twentieth century are now themselves semi-professional.

Finally, a word or two of caution on professional football. Such is the high profile of the sport that oral history can become confused and tales become taller the more they are passed on. Experience teaches that a talented footballing ancestor may well have been good at schoolboy level and/or have played for a local league side, but this can easily spiral via the jungle telegraph into his being a professional footballer or, equally favoured, 'having had trials' for a top professional club. The trials story is usually a safe one as there are few, if any, records of trialists and the tale can continue to be told as a family rumour. Trialists may have had a couple of run-outs in reserve matches and yet there may be no record of this. Suffice it to say that most professional club historians and programme editors reckon they would be wealthy men if they had £1 for every false trail they had been asked to follow in this respect.

As women's football teeters on the brink of semi-professionalism and professionalism in the early twenty-first century, it is interesting to note that there has been professional women's football in the past. Just after the First World War, rebuffed by the Football Association, the Dick, Kerr Ladies side went to the eastern seaboard of the United States, where they played nine professional games against men's teams: winning three, drawing three and losing three. They then returned to Britain where, as a writer in a popular weekly magazine later put it, they played 'on waste ground and village greens' (see The Amateurs chapter).

ATHLETICS

There can be little doubt that money played an important role in athletics during the sport's developmental years. In the late seventeenth century the sporty Charles II watched Lord Digby attempt to walk 5 miles in an hour on Newmarket Heath for a wager of £50. Members of the nobility also employed noted athletes in their households and used them in races against others similarly employed. These were known as 'running footmen' and a similar practice was to be found with cricketing noblemen and employees on their estates – especially gamekeepers.

By the early nineteenth century professional pedestrianism, race walking against the clock as well as against opponents, had become a huge spectator sport. Among its contestants were a number of men who had previously served as running footmen. Both betting and backing were involved and grounds were set up to host these events, which could, on occasions, last for a day or more. Stalls and beer tents were also established and the contests themselves recorded in diaries, songs and journals.

Due to the popularity of race walking, the names of many of the professional pedestrians are well known and recorded. One of the greatest was Foster Powell (1736–93) who came from Horsforth near Leeds in Yorkshire. His wagers ranged from 10 to 100 guineas per race and his feats were carried out on roads between London and York, involving both time and distance. Robert Bartley from Norfolk (born 1790) and Joseph Edge from Macclesfield were two other successful pedestrians.

In the first part of the nineteenth century, pedestrianism had strong military links and was seen as a good way of improving fitness before going on campaign. Although some of this activity could be described as amateur, there were those who also made money out of the sport. The most famous of these pedestrians was a Scot from Ury who raced under the name of Captain Barclay. His real name was Robert Barclay Allardice (1779–1854). One of the most outrageous challenges he took up was in 1807 when he successfully walked 1,000 miles in 1,000 hours for 1,000 guineas. He then joined his regiment as it left for active service in the Napoleonic Wars. He was one of the best known characters of his day and capable of attracting crowds of FA Cup final proportions. Other military pedestrians include Captains Howe and Hewetson, who walked 83 miles in less than 24 hours for a 200 guinea bet, and a Lieutenant Halifax of the Lancashire Regiment, who walked for 100 consecutive hours at 2 miles an hour near Tiverton in Devon.

Later in the century the best-known pedestrians included Charles Westall, George Davidson of Hoxton, Jemmy Miles of Brixton and George Littlewood of Sheffield. On Tyneside pedestrianism was incredibly popular and gave rise to a number of local heroes, including George Wilson. Slough, Liverpool and Manchester were other centres for the sport. Wales too had its stars and in February 1845 Welsh athlete John Davies (1822–c. 1904) defeated Sheffield coal carrier Tom Maxwell in a challenge at Lansdown near Bath.

By mid-century the general public had become bored with professional pedestrianism. As records became harder to break, the 'peds' turned to novelty races and competed carrying objects or racing against animals. Meanwhile, the audiences in the towns and cities were turning to events that were more exciting and took up less time. The age of the professional runner was about to begin. By the middle of the Victorian period track running had established itself in a number of centres. Lillie Bridge in London, Aston Lower Grounds in Birmingham and the Preston track all attracted large crowds, as did Powderhall in Edinburgh – a significant venue into the twentieth century – and numerous other grounds scattered around the north-east of England. Two runners in particular epitomised the professional era in running: Scotsman William Jaffray (1859–1919) and Englishman Walter George (1858–1943).

Paisley-born Jaffray began running as an amateur when young and stands as a good example of the stigma that could be attached to professionalism. When he turned professional as a teenager he changed his name to William Jeffrey Cummings in an apparent effort to save his family embarrassment. From the age of 14 Cummings, as he was then known, competed for purses between £10 and £100 over distances of 1, 4 and 10 miles. He was highly successful over each of these distances, returning such fast times that he came to the attention of English amateur runner Walter George.

Born in Wiltshire, George moved to the Midlands as a teenager and was enjoying running success similar to that of the Scot. Determined to take him on, he abandoned his amateur status and set up a series of meetings with Cummings. The first took place at Lillie Bridge with a reported 20,000 spectators in the grounds and another 30,000 locked out. George was victorious over the 1 mile distance. In front of a smaller crowd in Edinburgh, Cummings was victorious over 10 miles – a success he repeated over the same distance again in London. His time there stood as a record for well over a decade.

In the north-east of England the runners were revered and their names appeared frequently in the songs and ballads of the day (see How to Research Sporting Ancestors chapter). Foot racing was recorded in Preston,

Lancashire as early as 1675 and professional running from 1859, with a Highland Gathering at the Borough Gardens. Here it is recorded 'traditional Scottish sports' were carried out, including a foot race of half a mile for men in kilts. Preston then became a key venue for professional athletics. Powderhall in Edinburgh remained a significant home to professional athletics well into the twentieth century. Its open New Year 110m handicap (known universally as The Powderhall or The Big Sprint) was run there from 1870 to 1999 and had a large money prize. The ground later played host to greyhound racing and speedway. It is no longer in existence.

This Scottish link is perhaps unsurprising as professional sport – or the offer of prize money for sporting events – has long been an aspect of Highland Games, with tossing the caber and other 'field sports' also carried out for cash prizes (see below).

BILLIARDS

The great popularity of televised snooker in the late twentieth century disguises the fact that billiards, considered relatively boring as a spectator sport, had already enjoyed a lengthy and successful life as both a professional and amateur sport. It was a favourite of Prince Albert, the prince consort (d. 1862), and was played in the games rooms of the wealthy as well as the back rooms of public houses. Some even made a living as 'billiard markers' – a profession acknowledged by both Victorian and Edwardian census takers.

The first man attested to have made a living from playing billiards is Edwin (sometimes known as Jonathan) Kentfield. He was champion for well over twenty years during the early nineteenth century, a time when challenges of up to 100 guineas per match were not uncommon.

The World Professional Billiards Championships began in 1870 and the early years were dominated by the Roberts family – John Snr and John Jnr (1847–1919). John Jnr also made his name as a manufacturer of billiard tables and equipment. He was one of those responsible for setting up the Billiards Association in the 1880s and for organising and clarifying the game's rules and regulations. He was referred to as the 'W.G. Grace of billiards'. William Cook and Charles Dawson were two other names from the early years of the professional world championships.

One of the most successful of players in the early twentieth century was Melbourne Inman. In the 1881 census he appears aged 2 and living in Twickenham with his father Richard, who is described as a 'professor of billiards'. Still in Twickenham in 1901, aged 22 and now giving his name as 'Mel', his own professional entry is illegible but two of his brothers are described as 'billiard markers'.

Female involvement in the sport and in the UK championships can both be dated to the 1930s. In the second half of the twentieth century, television decreed that professional snooker was easier on the eye than billiards and for a number of years that sport enjoyed enormous popularity.

Boat Racing or Aquatics

Professional boat racing enjoyed considerable public support for most of Victoria's reign – especially in areas close to participating rivers such as the Thames, Tyne, Clyde and other waters like Loch Lomond. The development of railways from the 1830s onwards opened the sport up to wider audiences and, in some cases, special trains were put on to follow races for the entire length of the course.

Boat racing allowed for an archetypal division between those with money and leisure time to row as amateurs and those who were working men, employed in and around a river. For the latter a cash incentive was the highly valued Doggett's Coat and Badge. This, 'the oldest annual event in the English Sporting Calendar', was brought to the Thames in 1716 by Thomas Doggett, a Dublin-born actor who had made his way on the London stage. He introduced the competition in order to celebrate the coming to the English throne of the House of Hanover. The competition was between six watermen out of their apprenticeship. By the twentieth century amateurs were able to enter too, with the ability to opt out of the money prize in order to retain their amateur status.

Although the sport of professional aquatics is most closely associated with Victoria's reign, there had already been a groundswell of support for it in the years before the queen came to the throne. In his *Sketches of Boz*, written in 1836, Dickens noted of a Thames regatta:

A very lively and interesting scene. The river is studded with boats of all sorts, kinds and descriptions; places in the coal-barges at different wharfs [sic] are let to crowds of spectators, beer and tobacco flow freely about; men, women and children wait for the start in breathless expectation; cutters of six and eight oars glide gently up and down, waiting to accompany their protégés during the race.

By far the most popular of races were the single sculls, which were dominated during the great years by rowers from the Thames and the Tyne. Three of the great Thames scullers were Robert (Bob) Coombes (1808–60), Henry Kelley and Joseph Henry (Joe) Sadler.

Bob Coombes was a waterman and belonged to a guild that had been responsible for carrying passengers on the Thames for centuries. He and his fellows dominated the early years of professional rowing in the 1840s. As with many of these oarsmen, Coombes' funeral was a huge affair and his memorial tombstone a magnificent one. It stands in Brompton Cemetery in London, well over 6ft high and guarded by figures of watermen. On the top is a carving of his boat with his waterman's coat lying on top of it.

Henry Kelley was world champion in the 1860s but lost it to Tynesider Bob Chambers. He then helped the Australian Edward Trickett in his preparations to challenge for the world crown and taught him how to successfully use the new sliding seat. Kelley also took part in crewed races – most famously in a four-oared contest against the Canadians racing out of St John's, Brunswick in 1871.

Joe Sadler won the world championship in the 1870s before losing it to Trickett (Canadians and Australians were both fierce challengers for the world crown). Sadler had a reputation as a hard man determined to win at all costs – a reputation acknowledged by friend and foe alike. As the nineteenth century progressed, the watermen's work began to suffer as travellers started to use the new bridges that had been built across the river.

Many races were rowed on the River Clyde and Loch Lomond, with Scottish champion Robert Campbell much supported by his fellow countrymen. However, the greatest rivals to the Thames men were to be found on the River Tyne. Tyneside-born Henry (Harry) Clasper (1812–70) was the father of professional boat racing and also helped to develop the technology of the sport. Upon his retirement enough money was raised to buy him a public house and the Tyneside anthem, the *Blaydon Races*, was first performed at his testimonial dinner. Robert (Bob) Chambers (1831–68) was a favourite with the ladies, and became champion of the Thames, the Tyne and, eventually, the world. He died of consumption. James (Jim or Jimmy) Renforth (1842–71) collapsed during a race in Canada when a mixed four of Thames and Tyne men were taking on the Canadians. As he was dieing he lay cradled in the arms of sometime rival Henry Kelley, and likenesses of both men are represented on Renforth's Tyneside tombstone.

Other surnames that turned up in the sport during the great years of rowing include Robson, Hutton, Leithead, Grievson, Boyd, Elliot, Lumley, Cooper, Taylor, Scott, Thompson, Winship, Martin, Hammerton, Messenger, Hogarth and Wilson. Nearly all the rowers were tied to their local river in one way or another – usually working on or close by it, or by being born or living nearby. Most of the Thames professionals were watermen and belonged to a guild. Those on the Tyne were wherrymen or keelmen as well, ferrying the coal from the staithes to the sea-going vessels at the mouth of the river. Otherwise they worked in a local colliery or in one of the heavy industries situated on or close to the riverbanks. The replacement of the coal-carrying keelboats by railway trains had an effect on Tyneside rowing similar to that of the bridge building on the Thames on the London rowers.

As with other sports, rowing encompassed many different styles and spectatorial preferences. Some of the rowers were lightly muscled with long lithe strokes, while others were small, heavily muscled and pugnacious, with short but effective stabbing strokes. Of a race between two oarsmen, Candlish and McKenny, rowed in the 1850s, a ballad writer noted:

> The champion loved a lengthened stroke
> And skims along with grace
> McKenny's strokes are short and quick
> And rapid in their pace

Regattas attracted crowds fit to rival those attending top professional football matches today and also featured professional races with crews – two, four and eight oar in particular. The decline in professional boat racing matched the rise of association football, which is hardly surprising, and the round ball sport found passionate support; on Tyneside with Newcastle United and around the Thames with Fulham and Chelsea. With its enclosed ground and clear view of the entire event, football had an advantage over aquatics. Around the same time (1880s), professionals, including manual workers, as a whole were banned from taking part in what had previously been open boat races, which was another huge blow to the sport.

As with many of the sports that were attractive to betters and backers, professional boat racing was not free from skulduggery. In his *Boz* writings, Dickens refers to the boats full of backers and supporters who followed the race. By the middle of the century many of these were steamboats and there is evidence that such vessels were driven so close to an opponent's racing craft that the wash could put him off his stroke. There are also accounts of rowers 'cutting across their men' or driving them into the riverbank, whilst officials could be bribed to hold a boat back physically in order to give the other man an unfair advantage at the start.

Despite a decline in the sport's popularity, professional boat rowing continued well into the twentieth century and anecdotes were still being collected from former competitors until quite recently. In 2010, for example, an elderly gentleman informed a meeting of sports historians that his father had rowed in training with weights in his boat. This was to slow himself down as he knew that he was being both watched and timed by interested other parties standing on the riverbank. The canny rower was more than happy to give them a false impression of his capabilities. A local radio series on boat racing on Tyneside, which went out in the 1980s, produced a large postbag and evidence of considerable amounts of boat race memorabilia still surviving in private hands.

CRICKET

From the early days of recording cricket there has been a division between amateur and professional, between gentleman and player. They played together and for many years competed in a popular annual match against each other. When the hefty *Cricketers' Who's Who* was produced in the late twentieth century, its authors used this division for all who played first-class cricket from the publication of the first *Wisden* in the 1860s to the birth of the all-embracing term 'cricketer' in the 1960s. In theory, this division should make life easier for the family historian looking for cricketing ancestors. However (and as detailed in the introductory notes), the so-called amateur, supposedly so comfortably off that he had no need of wages, often made more out of the sport than the professional. This came as a result of general expenses demanded for appearances as well as the financial arrangements made for covering transport, meals and accommodation. A fine point, perhaps, yet one that needs to be made.

As long as cricket has been played there have been those who have benefited financially from their cricketing skills. John Small (1737–1826) played for the well-known Hambledon Club in Hampshire. He began as a shoemaker but later became a gamekeeper, and it was said that he often did a 7-mile round of woods and hatcheries before playing in a game. Thomas Taylor (1733–1800) was one of the best-known batsmen of his day and played for the White Conduit Club (started in the late eighteenth century and based in Islington, the club was important in the movement of the sport from the rural to urban environment). Taylor moved into gamekeeping from the pub business and was employed by the Duke of Bolton on his estate at Itchen Stoke. This was typical of the way professionalism worked in these days. The landed gentry often put out their own teams and played for wagers, using their estate workers as ringers. It should not cause disappointment, therefore, if research leads to the discovery of an alleged cricketing ancestor working on an eighteenth-century estate.

An interesting period in the professional game, and amateur too in terms of the opposition, came just before the first-class era when certain professional cricketers – most famously William Clarke and William Lilywhite – set up teams prepared to take on local sides 'against the odds'. There were a number of such sides during the 1840s and '50s such as the All England XI, a United All England XI and one other drawn from the South of England. In 1852 there was a game against Twenty Gentlemen of Hampshire and in 1846 against XX of Sheffield. In 1854, Clarke's XI took on a XXII of West Gloucestershire. Betting and backing were involved and the local side would often contain ringer professionals. The Australian tourists were still playing games against local amateurs and 'the odds' in the 1870s and '80s.

By this time the county structure was beginning to develop. Although sides were around in the Regency period playing under the names of Kent, Sussex, Essex and Hampshire, it is generally acknowledged that Sussex was the first permanent 'modern' county side, established in 1839.

Records for those who played professionally after 1864, especially at county level, are usually very good and can be found in a variety of places (see How and Where to Find Resources). A quick examination of some early specialist wicketkeepers provides some useful examples. Edward Gower Wenman (1803–79) was a regular for Kent and notoriously kept wicket without any protection while playing with one of the fastest bowlers of the day. He was also a slow underarm bowler and earned another living as a carpenter. Thomas Lockyer of Surrey (1826–69) is recognised as the first English wicketkeeper to have gone on a foreign cricketing tour – to North America then Australia. He was born and died in Croydon. Edward Pooley (1838–1907) played for Surrey on more than 200 occasions. He also toured with England. He was born in Richmond and died in a workhouse, but in 1871 he was living in Battersea with his family and is described as being a professional cricketer on the census return. Mordecai Sherwin (1851–1910) was born and died in Nottinghamshire and, like so many good sportsmen from the county, started life as a coal miner. He played over 200 games for his native county and three tests for England. He also kept goal for Notts County and stood as a parliamentary candidate.

As club cricket began to develop and to fit into a league structure towards the end of the Victorian period, the professional cricketer found another role and one that is still common today. He was often the only player in the side who was paid with the most common kind of club 'pro', an ex–first-class cricketer capable of coaching the youngsters and/or acting as groundsman. Some former first-class cricketers made a living from coaching alone – especially in the public schools (and the same applied to former professional runners and rowers). The pro's income usually consisted of a basic fee, bonuses for successful batting and wicket taking, plus the proceeds from benefit matches and occasional collections from spectators.

John Sherman (1788–1861) was the W.G. Grace of northern cricket with a career that lasted from 1809 to 1852. He acted as professional for the Manchester club towards the end of his career, but, born in Kent, he played most of his first-class cricket for Surrey. In 1851 he was living in Moss Lane, Hulme, Manchester and described as an engraver and calico maker. Ten years later, age 73, he was still in Manchester with his wife and four unmarried adult daughters – one a dressmaker, one a staymaker and two baby linen makers.

There were other kinds of pros too – youngsters on the verge of first-class cricket, for example. While touring the Isle of Wight with his club side in 1894, Somerset man John Mackie was hit all around the park by one Arthur Webb playing for the island's club side, Newport. Webb (1868–1952), then in his mid-20s, had been bought out of the King's Rifles by Hampshire and went on to open the batting for them. The pro could also be a local, a former amateur with a proven track record. In the 1920s Harry Coates,

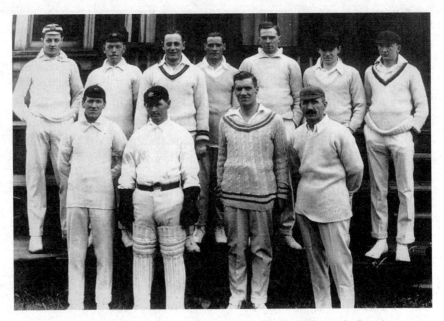

South Shields Cricket Club first XI, early 1920s. (Brian Pollard, Chester-le-Street)

a successful bat with Stockton Cricket Club, moved to nearby Saltburn as a professional. Top overseas cricketers were also employed as professionals – notably in the northern leagues. In some cases they married locally and settled in the area. The Lancashire leagues were famous for attracting West Indians in the twentieth century.

Despite the importance of first-class cricket, it would be unwise to assume that the club pro was always inferior to the first-class professional. The great England cricketer S.F. Barnes (1873–1967) did not like the first-class game and spent most of his career in the leagues in Lancashire and his native Staffordshire. He also played for minor county Staffordshire and took 189 test wickets for England.

After 1962 the notion of amateur and professional was discarded and all became cricketers The death had been a slow one. By 1950 professionals were allowed their initials on scorecards but printed after their surnames rather than before as in the case of amateurs. During that year, young professional Fred Titmus walked out in a first-class game at Lord's to a ringing announcement that the scorecard reference to 'F.J. Titmus' was inaccurate and should be altered to 'Titmus, F.J.'.

GOLF

The early history of golf appears in the chapter on amateurs, although it could equally have appeared here as money exchanged hands in games played in the seventeenth and eighteenth centuries. Sport historians now acknowledge the first true professional golfer to have been Scotsman Allan Robertson (1815–59). Robertson, whose father David was also heavily involved in the game, made a living from teaching golf, from participating in foursomes and individual 'private' games where money was at stake.

By the middle of the nineteenth century, Scotland had a number of professionals similar to Robertson. They played against each other at well-established courses such as St Andrews, Prestwick, Musselburgh and North Berwick. The brothers Dunn (Willie and James) and 'Old Tom' Morris were leading figures in the game at this point.

At this time there was also a cry for an effective multi-player competition. An inter-club competition was held at St Andrews in 1857 and was won by the English-based Royal Blackheath Club. This was followed by an attempt to establish an amateur competition at Prestwick, which collapsed after two years. This was followed in 1860 by a competition for professionals over the same course. The prize was a challenge belt and 30 guineas (a considerable sum in those days) and Willie Park of Musselburgh won it. In 1861 the competition was made 'Open to all the world', thus giving birth to the British Open. The contest rotated between St Andrews, Musselburgh and Prestwick at first, and the much-revered claret jug became the winner's reward. In the early years, the competition was dominated by the Morrises – 'Old Tom' and his son 'Young Tom' – and by the aforementioned Willie Park. Another well-known Scottish golfer was Willie Fernie (1857–1924) from St Andrews who won the Open in 1883. He was also runner-up in the Open Championship in 1882, 1884, 1890 and 1891.

South of the border, development came much more slowly. As late as 1880 there were only a dozen or so golf clubs in England. By 1914 this had risen to well over a thousand with something approaching a quarter of a million players involved. The vast majority was male, middle and upper class, and amateur – with the professionals attached individually to clubs and spending their time in caddying, looking after the greens, making clubs, teaching and playing in challenge matches.

HIGHLAND GAMES

One significant area inhabited by professional and semi-professional sports-men, and especially those of Scottish birth or descent, was the Highland Games. The profile of these games was raised considerably in the nineteenth century by royal interest with Braemar and Fort William being popular venues. They attracted competitors at hammer throwing and caber tossing, as well as wrestling and running. A major feature of the Fort William games was a race up Ben Nevis.

One of the best-known competitors at the Highland Games was Donald Dinnie (1837–1916), who is said to have won thousands of athletic events and to have competed up to the age of 70. Aberdeenshire-born, he died in London and became a wealthy man due to his success in a large number of sports – especially wrestling. He competed in Highland Games over a period of sixteen seasons and was considered by many at the time to be the greatest athlete of his day. The famous fiddler and tune writer J. Scott Skinner wrote a strathspey in his honour and his strength was acknowledged by the naming of heavy artillery shells after him in the First World War.

Annual sports in the English Lake District also drew in professional and semi-professional athletes. Perhaps the most famous of these are the Grasmere Sports with a guide race up a local fell, track and field athlet-ics, and Cumberland and Westmoreland wrestling. The roots of many of these sports are ancient but most of them became truly organised in the Victorian period and were opened up to competitors and spectators alike by the coming of the railways. In 1858 Charles Dickens called in at the Ferry Sports and Regatta at nearby Windermere and found, besides wres-tling, 'all sorts of other amusements; running matches, for a mile or so; dog trails; jumping matches', yet in his opinion 'the greatest of all treats' was 'the pole leaping'.

HORSE RACING

Although horse racing is a sport with a lengthy pedigree, it was not until the eighteenth century that it began to capture real public interest in Britain. Prior to this the main interest in horse racing was regal and noble. The Tudors' love of hunting led them to dabble in the sport. In the following century, James I seized on Newmarket as a centre for equine activity, though tracks still known today at Carlisle, Lincoln and Doncaster also began to put on race meetings. Chester was particularly significant during these early days. Charles II revived activity in the Newmarket area after the dull days of the Cromwellian Commonwealth, while Anne, the last of the Stuart monarchs, took a real interest in horse racing and set up Royal Ascot (1711) for racing purposes rather than fashion.

In general, the owners or their grooms rode the horses as the sport developed, so it is difficult to talk of professional jockeys as such in the early days. However, William Tregonwell Frampton, recognised as the first professional trainer of racehorses, was at work in the seventeenth century. Born in Oxfordshire in 1641, he arrived at Newmarket during the reign of Charles II. He became supervisor of the racehorses during the reign of William III and also keeper of the king's running horses – the latter post being held into the reign of Queen Anne.

One outcome of the early eighteenth-century explosion of interest was the establishment of many new racetracks. York was one such course. Details of races and results began to be recorded formally, although the actual racing was notoriously unregulated and the courses themselves not enclosed.

Horse racing was one of the first sports – if not *the* first – to become properly organised. The Jockey Club was founded in the middle of the eighteenth century and the racing calendar set up as a number of the classics got under way. The St Leger, The Oaks and The Derby were established by the end of the century with the 1,000 Guineas and 2,000 Guineas following in the early nineteenth century. By now, the word professional could be applied to many people involved in horse racing, including writers, trainers and administrators. Unfortunately for the family historian, the names of owners and horses were more likely to be recorded than those of the jockeys.

The first recognised successful professional jockey was Sam Chifney (1753–1807) – not to be confused with his son Sam Chifney Jnr (1786–1855) who was also successful in the business. Chifney Snr rode for the Prince Regent but, despite his successes, he acquired something of a reputation as a shady character. After one particular controversy he left the sport, still secure personally in financial terms. Yet he still managed to end his life in poverty at the age of 53. His son won The Derby twice on Sam (1818) and Sailor (1820). Working with his brother William, a trainer, Chifney Jnr both owned and rode many winners. He was well-off and lived in some style at Newmarket, winning his last classic in 1843 at the age of 57.

Frank Buckle (1766–1832) was another leading jockey of the day. He won The Oaks nine times between 1797 and 1823, and had his portrait painted on a number of occasions. He was a popular jockey and respected for his intelligence. All in all he was also the most successful classic jockey until Lester Piggott in the twentieth century. Members of the day, the Edwards and Goodison families, were also successful jockeys.

As the nineteenth century progressed, so did an interest in steeplechasing, which later came to rival the existing racing on the flat in terms of interest. Point-to-point racing was around by the 1830s, as was steeplechasing with its own local rules. St Albans was an early jumps racecourse, along with Cheltenham and Liverpool (with racing at Maghull first and Aintree later). Racing at both Cheltenham and Liverpool was well under way before Victoria came to the throne in 1837. The Flat Jockeys Championship was set up in the middle of the nineteenth century while The National Hunt Jockey Championship dates from 1900 (see The Amateurs chapter). Elnathan Flatman (1810–60) dominated the flat in the late 1840s and '50s. So well was he known that he was often referred to in the press as Nat. He was followed by George Fordham (1837–87) who was in control from the mid-1850s to the early '60s. The punters soon lost sight of his glorious achievements: on his deathbed, he claimed that he had been forgotten by the masses and was glad for the few friends who were gathered around him.

Frederick James Archer (1857–86), known simply as Fred, was perhaps the most famous Victorian jockey. He was Cheltenham-born and won his first race at the age of 12. He was victorious in The Derby on five occasions and champion jockey for thirteen consecutive years. A tall man for a jockey, he struggled to keep his weight down and, suffering depression after the death of his wife, committed suicide at a very early age. Another character was Jem Snowden (1844–89), who won four classics during Victorian times. He was known for his drinking and inability to turn up for races on time.

By 1881 professionals involved in the sport were making a good living and returns from the census that year show that many jockeys and trainers were able to afford servants. Clerks of the course may also be of interest. Sports historian Mike Huggins reveals in an article on nineteenth-century horse racing that Thomas Sotheran, a York bookseller and stationer, was clerk of the course at his local racecourse, while Joseph Lockwood, an alderman, held a similar post at Doncaster. By the late Victorian period race-going was also more controlled as the courses gradually came to be enclosed.

Despite enjoying an element of financial security and regarded by many as Britain's leading sport at the time, professional horse racing was not at its best in the late Victorian period. Some of the earlier racecourses had already closed – such as Derby and Preston – and many modern town and city maps note the sites of 'the old racecourse'. In Birmingham, for example, the sites of over forty racetracks are known and not a single one is still operative today. More significant still was the growing opposition to the sport because of its reputation for betting and for 'loose behaviour' at race meetings. Non-conformist religious movements and teetotal organisations seized on horse racing in particular as respectability became the order of the day. Despite this, many people still made a good living out of the sport in the twentieth century.

Although boasting many 'amateurs' in its early days, steeplechasing/National Hunt racing had its seasonal championship dominated by professionals in the twentieth century. Particularly successful in Edwardian times was Frank 'Tich' Mason. (See The Amateurs chapter for more on racing over fences).

PRIZEFIGHTING, BOXING & PUGILISM

As Julian Norridge noted in his book *How the British Invented Sport*, fisticuffs as a sport has a lengthy history, or rather, 'boxing began when the first person raised his fist in play or in anger'. In terms of the history of British boxing, bare-knuckle fights were certainly the order of the day by the close of the seventeenth century – if in a disorganised and unregulated way. The sport continued to blossom in the eighteenth and early nineteenth century, with respectability and legal recognition coming to it in the late nineteenth century. Today it is recognised as the first British sport to have a set of recognisable rules (1740s).

Information on pugilists from the early days is also quite full, mainly because of the sport's popularity. Its supporters were known in a group as The Fancy; mainly men drawn from different social and economic classes. They were united by a love of danger and betting, and a boxing crowd might have included anyone from an underground criminal to a peer of the realm. As the nineteenth century progressed, all interested were able to keep up with events through the developing sporting press.

Oxfordshire-born James Figg is generally recognised as the first great English prizefighter. He was champion in the 1720s and '30s and also excelled at fencing. Two other early champions were Daniel Mendoza (1764–1836) and Tom Cribb (1781–1848). Mendoza ruled as the Champion of All England and wrote a book on the art of boxing. He was relatively small and slight for a fighter in the days when there was no division of weights. Upon retirement he opened his own boxing academy.

Cribb remains a legend in boxing. One of his most famous bouts was fought in 1810 against Tom Molineaux, an American former slave who had come to Britain while employed as a sailor. Cribb was victorious and his success brought his sponsor, the pedestrian Captain Barclay, an estimated £10,000. Although he also worked in London as a coal porter, Cribb was a Bristolian by birth and Bristol proved a fertile breeding ground for many of the early prizefighters. These included Jem Belcher, Hen Pearce and coal hewer Ben Brain. Belcher's brother Tom was also a respected prize fighter. Jem was blind by the age of 22 and dead by 30. This was a tough sport.

One problem faced by those researching early prizefighters lies in the use of stage, or rather ring, names by some of these fighters. The popular Tom Spring was actually christened Tom Winter, while Bendigo was a name adopted by Nottingham fighter William Thompson. It was apparently a family nickname given to him when he was a child. Thompson spent some time in the workhouse in his youth and was a gifted athlete – equally adept at running, gymnastics, throwing and cricket.

There is much interest in the early history of boxing and articles appear in history magazines, including family history magazines which have recently featured articles on the contest between Bill Neat and Hickman 'The Gas Man' in 1821. This took place on Hungerford Common and was a particularly bloody fight. Bill Neat was one of the 'Bristol Boys' and eighteen rounds were fought in front of a crowd of over 20,000. Another famous contest was between England's Tom Spring and Ireland's Jack Langan in 1824.

Pugilism was also considered exciting because of its brushes with the law. Rings for individual fights were put up and taken down swiftly, and most fights took place in the open countryside, close to county borders where possible, in order to confuse the police. In 1841 Dick Cain, aged 22, fought against Ned Adams, aged 19, on the fringes of Bedfordshire. The contest between Cribb and Molineaux took place in rural Leicestershire in front of a crowd of 20,000.

Many of these fights took place before the railways were in place so spectators must have made a considerable effort to get there. Once the railways were running, the railway companies would put on last minute 'specials' in order to take supporters to their destination. Fight promoters did not have it their own way, however, and at one point the authorities in Surrey took a stand against the sport and prosecuted the organisers of one contest.

As was the case with a number of other professional nineteenth-century sports, supporters were generous towards pugilists when their careers came to an end and would organise whip-rounds or benefits. Many ex-boxers bought into the pub business and some of them suffered the consequences. Some took to alcohol even if they did not become landlords, and there were always supporters that were prepared to buy drinks in return for a chat about 'the old days'. Cribb lost the pub he bought on a horse race bet. Bendigo, on the other hand, turned to evangelist religion after struggling with the demon drink. Other pugilists continued to earn money by joining travelling fairs and taking on all-comers for financial reward in the booths. This was a thankless job, often leading to permanent physical and mental damage.

The Knock Out!

'Sport in the Armed Forces', *The Bystander's Fragments from France*, Vol. 7 (1919). (Author's collection)

Sparring and training sessions enjoyed public support too and there is a fine sketch of one such well-attended session at the Fives Court, St James Street in London's Haymarket.

Another way of following the story of professional boxing is through the changes in the laws governing the sport. In the early days, rules suggested by John Broughton were adopted. Broughton was an early eighteenth-century waterman and rower, and his laws remained at the heart of boxing for a century. Thanks to him the term 'up to the mark' and 'up to scratch' have entered common parlance. He died in 1789 and was buried in Westminster Abbey. In 1750, while he was alive, Parliament affirmed that the sport was still illegal.

For the first half of Victoria's reign, the London Prize Ring Rules held sway and many of the most famous bare-knuckle fights were fought under this regime. Respectability (or perceived respectability) came into being in the years following the adoption of the Marquis of Queensberry's Rules in 1867. Rightly or wrongly, the marquis and his rules have entered the language as by-words for 'fair play'.

One of the major developments of the late Victorian period was the use of gloves in contests. The idea was not brand new and lightweight gloves had been used before – especially in sparring. Boxing as we know it gradually came into existence as different weight categories were established; at first heavyweight, middleweight and lightweight. Bantamweight and featherweight divisions were set up in the 1890s. Other weights such as flyweight, welterweight and light heavyweight were introduced in the twentieth century.

British success at world level came very slowly, although there was a bantamweight world champion bout in London in the 1890s. Only one British boxer held the World Heavyweight Championship in the first century of competition, Cornishman Bob Fitzsimmons (1863–1917). American boxer John L. Sullivan, who won the championship under London Prize Ring Rules, was actually Irish-born. Britain enjoyed greater success at lightweight, with Scottish, Welsh and Irish boxers featuring prominently. Freddie Welsh (1886–1927) was the name adopted in the ring by Welshman Frederick Hall Thomas. He was World Lightweight Champion before the First World War. Cardiff-born Jim Driscoll (1880–1925) won British, European and world titles at featherweight. He died of pneumonia.

The search for boxing ancestors may prove particularly fruitful in the years between the two wars. In industrial towns and cities in particular, recession encouraged many young men to take up the sport in order to make money. Rings were set up in welfare halls and special arenas were established in some areas. Boxing events here often had long cards and large audiences, and the more successful boxers became and remain local folk heroes. Their deeds are frequently recalled in articles in local and regional newspapers and magazines.

RUGBY

Professional rugby exists in Britain today in two forms: Rugby Union and Rugby League. It was not always thus as the professional sport of Rugby Union is a child of the late twentieth century. Those seeking out professional rugby-playing ancestors must therefore look to Rugby League from the 1890s onwards. Prior to this date there was simply amateur rugby, which was often known as football in those days – even after association football came into existence in the 1860s.

For most of Victoria's reign rugby football remained, in theory, an amateur sport, but many of the northern clubs, boasting large crowds and eager for success, became concerned at the loss of earnings suffered by their players. Many of these players worked in the local mills and factories and a 'broken time' payment was not considered out of order. This could be paid for time spent both in training and in playing.

Other clubs disagreed with this approach and talk was of a divide between the prosperous south and the less prosperous north (although the less prosperous north-east of England stayed with the amateur game). In addition, the northern clubs were eager to move the game on by creating a league structure. Friendlies and cup matches alone were not enough, and league rivalry would increase public interest. This went against the Corinthian spirit of the gentleman's game.

In 1895 the breakaway sides formed the Northern Union (which did not take up the title of the Rugby League until the 1920s). There were twenty-two sides in the new union initially; twelve from Yorkshire, nine from Lancashire and one from Cheshire. A sure indicator of the reasons for the split can be seen in the fact that the on-pitch laws of the game changed little at first. Today, many of the differences between union and league are instantly recognisable: fifteen players in union, thirteen in league; line outs in union, none in league; unlimited tackling in union, limited tackling in league.

Professional Rugby League ancestors are likely to be found in the two largest northern counties, Yorkshire and Lancashire. The final of the Northern Union Challenge Cup was first held at Leeds in 1897. Batley won the first two finals with Huddersfield described in sporting histories as the most famous name from the early league days. Huddersfield's Albert Rosenfeld scored a record-breaking eighty tries in the season before the First World War, and in the following season the team won all four cups available under the guidance of Harold Wagstaff. In 1921 Harold Buck became the first £1,000 signing. New clubs sprang up specifically to play league. Bramley was formed by a vicar in 1896.

Some of the early clubs such as Tyldesley, Liversedge, Manningham and Brighouse Rangers are now defunct. Another former club, Broughton Rangers, enjoyed some success during its years in existence, while Manningham of Bradford won the first Northern Union Championship in 1896. Runcorn had a league club between 1895 and 1914 and a number of players received the call-up to play for the national side. These included J. Butterworth, S. Walker (1905) and A. Kennedy (1911). Runcorn's Jim Jolley won Rugby League caps for England and Great Britain during the Edwardian period, as did Dick Padbury, who was still playing for England in 1912. Sam Houghton also won an England cap while playing for Runcorn in the days before the split.

By the end of the nineteenth century significant cup competitions were in place. Yorkshire and Lancashire had their own discrete Challenge Cups from Edwardian times, and clubs from the west Cumbrian coast soon helped to increase the numbers of players involved in the professional game.

Not all of the defunct sides were lost to sport completely. Two Bradford sides, Manningham (playing Rugby League 1895–1903) and Bradford (1864–1907), switched codes completely. Manningham became Bradford City AFC and Bradford became Bradford Park Avenue AFC. Bradford City remains a Football League side today.

Those with Welsh rugby playing ancestry may also find success in looking into the history of Welsh Rugby League sides that were in existence just before the First World War. These include Aberdare, Barry, Ebbw Vale, Merthyr Tydfil and Mid Rhondda. These sides produced Welsh Rugby League internationals such as Oliver Burgham of Barry, who also played for Great Britain, as did Dai 'Tarw' Jones of Merthyr.

The professional structure of Rugby League is not as straightforward as it first seems. When the league was formed, officials argued that they were legalising what had already been taking place before and had previously been regarded as 'subterfuge and deception' – a subterfuge and deception which, some argued, continued as shamateurism in some areas of Rugby Union. In essence, it did not become a full-time professional sport as players were paid by the game and not at all during the close season or if under suspension. For many years the vast majority of Rugby League players had other jobs. One Barrow superstar of the pre-war era worked as an electrician and caused havoc among the ladies of the GPO Telephone Exchange when he came to fix the lights. Similarly, the Welsh James brothers were employed as warehousemen.

WRESTLING

An internet search for ancestral professional wrestlers may lead down a number of interesting blind alleys. Websites on the late twentieth-century boom in 'theatrical' American wrestling are very common. So too are references to those involved in the staged popular televised British sport of the 1960s and '70s. However, continued patience should eventually produce information on a sport which had existed in numerous different guises in different regions of Britain from the nineteenth century and before. This sport, in its own way, produced as many local heroes as boxing did.

Wrestling was a popular money-earning sport in south-west and north-west England and Scotland. Its origins were said to be Celtic though one area of north-west England claims that its style was introduced by the Vikings – and wrestling was essentially about style. Working from the south upwards, the main styles were: Cornish, Devon, Lancashire, Cumberland and Westmoreland (more recently Cumbrian), and Scottish back hold. The first two styles had much in common, as did the last two, which were often placed together under the 'North Country' heading.

One of the stars of Cornish wrestling was James Polkinghorne (b. 1788). He was a publican from St Columb Major and is remembered for his involvement in a contest with Devonian Abraham Cann. The contest was adjudged to be a draw. Richard Parkyn (*c.* 1772–1853) was another well-known Cornish wrestler. He lived in the same area as Polkinghorne and was born on the cusp of three parishes. His eventual fame led each parish to claim him for their own. In 1811, Parkyn took part in a contest against the cream of Devon alongside other Cornish wrestlers. *The Sporting Magazine* of the day gave a brief account of events, which went the way of the Cornish. Although the word amateur was used in the article, its author ended by noting that 'the Cornish gentlemen offered, in answer to a bet offered at Crediton, to get ten Cornish men who should play against the same number of Devonshire men for any sum, from one hundred to a thousand pounds'.

There was no doubt that wrestling was popular, that bets were cast and that money changed hands. In 1811 the Marquis of Queensbury and Lord Lonsdale were among a crowd of 12,000 people who watched the wrestling, Cumberland and Westmoreland style, at Carlisle races (unlike the physical county of Westmorland, the wrestling style retained the 'e' in its name). When Polkinghorne took on Cann at Tamar Green near Devonport, a similar crowd was in attendance with a purse of £400 (£200 aside) available to the winner.

Cumberland and Westmoreland wrestling was very popular in the area in and around the English Lake District during the early and mid-nineteenth century, and many of the sport's great wrestlers were mentioned in the songs and ballads of the day (see the How to Research Sporting Ancestors chapter). Among these were Thomas Longmire, Richard Wright, Robert Atkinson and William Jackson. In 1851 Atkinson of Sleagill, Westmorland met Jackson of Kinneyside, Cumberland for the championship of England. The contest, for a purse of £300, attracted an estimated 10,000 spectators. A contemporary street ballad refers to 'The Championship of England and £300 in gold' and also to the spectators who had travelled from Whitehaven, Penrith, Carlisle and Newcastle (by then the Newcastle to Carlisle railway had been running for a few years). So popular was the Cumbrian wrestler Thomas Longmire that a biography was published in 1887.

Lancashire wrestling claims to have been at the root of many of the developments in twentieth-century professional wrestling on both sides of the Atlantic. One of the best known wrestlers here was Tom Cannon who moved to the USA and changed style slightly to make the sport more exciting. It has been noted recently that this form of wrestling, also known in its early days as 'catch-as-catch-can', created few written records. Like potshare bowling in north-east England, it was a working-class sport and of little interest to the readers of Victorian newspapers and magazines. Fights often took place on the slag banks of the Lancashire coalfields with a hat passed round for collecting money and the winner taking all.

Another popular wrestler in this area was 'Little Joe' Acton (1852–1917), who competed in England and the USA during the late nineteenth century. He defeated Cannon in 1881 to become the first World Heavyweight Champion. The legendary Scottish strongman Donald Dinnie (of Highland Games fame) was an outstanding wrestler and won his first professional prize in the sport at the age of 16. Scottish back wrestling for cash prizes was very popular at the Highland Games, although participating wrestlers were later excluded with the move towards Olympic participation nearing the end of the nineteenth century.

OTHER PROFESSIONAL SPORTS OF INTEREST

Swimming enjoyed professionalism at a number of times in its development. In the early nineteenth century, professional swimmers were known as professors and indulged in a number of swimming activities. The Beckwiths were a key family in this area. Frederick Beckwith cast himself as Professor Beckwith of Lambeth Baths and arranged many competitions – some one-on-ones, some against the clock and some over distance. In many of these contests he involved his son (William) and his daughter. The National Swimming Society was established in 1837 and the Professional Swimming Association in 1881. By the time Beckwith organised an 'aquatic entertainment' for the royal family towards the end of the century, the move was clearly towards amateur swimming.

Earlier reference has been made to the importance of professional boat racing on the Thames and Tyne. Betting and backing made other 'regional' sports popular too. On Tyneside again, the sport of potshare bowling attracted large crowds. This sport relied entirely on strength and was similar in some ways to putting the shot. Young strong coal miners were the main protagonists and much money was laid out in betting and backing. The more common game of bowls also attracted wagers in its very early days.

Big money was also to be earned in the Fenland area of Norfolk and Cambridgeshire where ice-skating held sway during the winter months of the mid-nineteenth century. This sport produced great characters with fine sounding names. One was Turkey Smart, born 1830 as William Smart. An agricultural labourer with a large family to feed, he was dominant in the 1850s and was capable of earning the equivalent of two years' salary in one successful race. Larman Register, son of a farmer and later a farmer himself, was another success, as were members of the Drake and Fish families.

Professional dog racing did not evolve until the 1920s. In terms of motorised sport, the prestigious TT motorcycle races have been going since 1907. The first Motor Grand Prix was held in 1906 and there was little British involvement until much later (though Henry Segrave was victor in the Grand Prix in 1923).

THE AMATEURS

A vast number of sports come under the amateur umbrella. As with professional, the word amateur is not easy to define satisfactorily and has been
used here to describe sport which was played mainly for pleasure rather
than for financial reward. One or two of the less popular sports may have
been left out, but the aim is to cover as many of the influential amateur
British sports as space will allow. A separate Olympic section is included at
the end of the chapter.

ARCHERY

The history of archery stretches back to medieval times both in fact and in
legend – to the archers of Agincourt and to fireside tales of Robin Hood
and his archery contests. From the seventeenth century onwards it was very
strong in Scotland in the shape of the Royal Company of Archers, described
today as a private club with an important ceremonial function as part of the
monarch's bodyguard in Scotland. The company's members came mainly
from the nobility and its history is dealt with in detail in a number of books
and online encyclopaedic sites.

The eighteenth century proved significant in terms of the organisation
of the sport in England. In 1780 Lancastrian Sir Ashton Lever formed the
Toxophilite Society, an organisation that was to receive the royal seal of

approval seven years later. In the middle of the nineteenth century competitive archery began to attract an even wider audience. An important meeting
was held at York in the 1840s and a club was formed in Cheltenham in 1857.
During the same decade, an important competition was held at Leamington
in the Midlands. By the 1860s there were national archery contests and these
proved a moveable feast as shown by the venues between 1881 and 1909:

> Sutton Coldfield, 1886; Bath, 1887; Cheltenham 1888; York; 1889; Oxford
> 1890; Southampton, 1891; Worcester, 1892; Eastbourne, 1895; Hurlington,
> 1898; Oxford, 1899; Brighton, 1900; Edgbaston, 1902; Clifton, 1903;
> Edinburgh, 1904; Great Malvern, 1905; Southampton, 1906; Oxford, 1907;
> York, 1908; Oxford, 1909.

The driving force behind the Cheltenham club was Horace Alfred Ford,
regarded by many as the greatest target archer of all time. His interest in
archery dates back to the 1840s and he won the national championship
on twelve occasions (eleven of them consecutively). Born in London
in 1822, he later worked as a colliery manager. In retirement he lived in
Gloucestershire and wrote books about the art of archery.

Archery is regarded as one of the first organised sports to have involved
women in large numbers. The most successful female archer of the day
was Alice Legh, who dominated the women's sport for some thirty years
during the late Victorian and post-First World War period. She came from
a wealthy family and though Canadian-born was of British parentage. She
was in her mid-20s when she won her first national title and went on to
take more than twenty national titles over a span of four decades. Her thun-
der was stolen somewhat by Sybil 'Queenie' Newall, who took the gold
medal at the 1908 London Olympics (see the Olympic section of this chapter the Case Studies chapter). Legh did not enter the Olympics but defeated
Newall in competition a few days after the Games ended.

ASSOCIATION FOOTBALL

Such is the high standing of professional football in the early twenty-first
century that the amateur game is often looked down upon or ignored. This
should not be the case, and certainly not when looking out for ancestral

footballers. As football and family history expert Colin Dean noted in 2004, 'almost all able bodied men since 1880 have played the game at some time'. What is more, there is a mass of surviving records to prove it.

Unlikely as it may seem, those who enjoyed success in the ancient Shrovetide foot-ball games, or folk football as it is sometimes called, may have left records. Songs and ballads about some of these games have survived from the nineteenth century and the games themselves were often recorded in the local press. If the family has a story about a past member scoring a goal, or 'hale', in such a game it may be worth following up. Goals were rare in such games and the scorer was often regaled as a local hero (in one part of the town or village at least).

In theory, all footballers were amateur from the acknowledged birth of the game in 1863 to the formation of the Football League in 1888 (see The Professionals chapter for well-founded doubts on this theory). The concept of amateurism was particularly strong in the wealthier south of England and in Presbyterian Scotland. Thus 18-year-old centre forward John Petrie, who scored thirteen goals in Arbroath's record breaking 36–0 win over Bon Accord in 1885, was recorded as an amateur.

The early footballers who played for amusement alone have left little in the way of records. In the 1870s and early '80s rugby football held sway in many areas and the local press did not give football (association) much in the way of coverage. In most cases only surnames or scorers' surnames were provided and these were often misspelt. There were no match programmes, few records and games were only local cup games or friendlies. Local cup finals and FA Cup games tended to receive wider press coverage than other games. Sports historian Ian Nannestad notes that Scotland presents a particular problem when it comes to early records, with players often referred to in the press simply as 'new man' or 'trialist'.

Many of the teams that were to enjoy success in the 'professional era' came into existence in the 'amateur era'. Their club histories may be useful to the family historian although, in terms of early records, the club historian also has little to work on. The clubs that remained amateur and dominated this period have their histories – in particular Oxford University, Wanderers and Old Etonians. These sides featured heavily in the early FA Cup and the names of players involved can be picked up from a variety of sources. An England side of the 1890s included amateurs from Oxford University, Cambridge University and Corinthians, and those selected had their initials in front of their names while the professionals had their surnames alone printed.

School football captains in *The Boy's Own Paper*. (Author's collection)

Among the first star amateurs was Robert Walpole Sealy Vidal. Born in Devon in 1853, he went to Westminster School and entered the Church. He played for the Wanderers and for England, competed in FA Cup finals and on one occasion, in the days when the scoring side took the next kick-off, scored three goals without the opponents touching the ball. There was also Alexander Bonsor, born Surrey in 1851, who played for the Wanderers and the Old Etonians, and scored one of the first international goals. Bonsor (later a brewer), his Belgium-born wife and his servant were staying at the Grand Hotel in London at the time of the 1881 census.

In 1885 a team of 'plumbers and weavers' playing for Blackburn Olympic made unexpected progress in the FA Cup. The astonished amateurs of the south looked into the make-up of the side and discovered two unexpected recent imports from Scotland. The first southern side to turn professional was the Royal Arsenal in 1891 and the Corinthian spirit remained strong – literally. In 1894, the amateur Corinthians side supplied all eleven of the England team, which took on Wales and remained a significant side well into the twentieth century. As part of the constant confusion between amateur and professional, historian Mike Huggins noted that generous expenses had made the Corinthians 'a professional side in all but name' by 1889. The amateur Isthmian and Athenian Leagues were also very strong for many years.

In the year that the Corinthians provided the entire England side, a separate amateur cup was inaugurated. Old Carthusians, Dulwich Hamlet and Clapton enjoyed early success in the competition, which also enjoyed enormous popularity with fans and players in the Durham coalfields. As late as the 1950s, teams such as Bishop Auckland and Crook Town enjoyed national reputations while West Auckland famously won a 'World Cup' in the early twentieth century – an event that ended up dramatised in both a television drama and a stage play. Pegasus Football Club also flew the flag for the university-trained amateurs during this later period.

For the vast majority of keen amateurs, football was played in the Church leagues and Wednesday leagues. Some historians suggest that they were seen by organisations as a way of soaking up surplus energy with many religious bodies and factories/works keen to promote the sport. The Sunday leagues, increasingly popular as the twentieth century progressed, found little favour in the early days due to religious objections. In fact, the FA banned them until the 1920s. The extent of this type of football is quite staggering. While celebrating its Golden Jubilee in 1955, the Birmingham and District Works Amateur Football Association was able to name 677 sides that had been members at one time or another. Among these were Abingdon Echo (from 1908), Ingall Parsons Clive and Company (1909) and Muntz Metal (1907).

Those who turned out in these leagues played for the teams like the GPO, Co-op, Boys' Brigade or a works' side. Southampton Football Club, still nicknamed The Saints today, started life as a church team. Hibernian, the Edinburgh side, was formed from members of a Catholic church in 1875. Crewe Alexandra was the brainchild of railway workers who met at the Alexandra pub. Some sides were formed at sports clubs already in existence, with Preston North End developing from Preston Cricket Club. Others developed from old boys' clubs (i.e. clubs formed by young men who had played at school together). This was the case with cricket and rugby, too.

The Edwardian and inter-war periods were particularly fruitful for this kind of football, which was often covered by the local press. Family historian Anthony Clarke from Alcester, Worcester researched his paternal grandfather, Alfred (b. 1884), who played for Arrow FC in Warwickshire around 1906. Anthony discovered that Alfred had been a left-back and found some of his games covered by the local newspaper. In a nice link to the study of professional football, there was a family story of unsuccessful trials with Wolves (Wolverhampton Wanderers) but, as might be expected, no written confirmation of the experience.

The amateur footballer came into his own in wartime when, with the professional game suspended, both organised and ad hoc games took place for those in uniform and those on civvy street. These games are often the subject of family tales and there are records and memorabilia to back this up, though the sport was obviously less organised and dependable than in peacetime. It is, however, a popular area for research and a number of books and booklets have been published on the subject. Here it is not unusual to find the Wednesday afternoon amateurs taking to the field with professionals and even internationals – and, naturally, proud of it (see the author's family case study for many of the issues raised in this section).

The history of women's football is another area that is attracting increasing interest. In 1895 one women's football match in London drew 10,000 spectators, but in 1902 women's football was banned by the FA. Photographs, newspaper reports and other memorabilia suggest that the ban did not work. Women's amateur football had to face consistent male opposition. In 1894 Nettie Honeyball founded the British Ladies Football Club and football enjoyed some currency until 1902, when the Football Association banned its members from playing against ladies' teams. In 1895 the ladies played games across the country and attracted large crowds but, as historians have observed, the 'novelty wore off'. Nettie herself remains something of a mystery and her name may even have been a pseudonym.

Always enjoying support in and around the factories of the north of England, ladies' football saw a large increase in interest during the First World War. There are a number of examples of teams developing in and around factories set up during the war. One of the most studied is the Dick, Kerr Ladies side. Set up in Preston, this side played numerous games in support of funds for injured soldiers (the players were given 'expenses' of 10 shillings a game to cover loss of earnings) and also participated in internationals against the French side. Women's football continued its popularity after the war and in 1920 their cup final attracted a crowd of 53,000 to Goodison Park, Liverpool with thousands more locked out. Such popularity began to panic the Football Association and in 1921 it banned female use of member pitches. The Dick, Kerr Ladies side enjoyed a brief period of professionalism in the USA and continued to play in the Preston area until the 1960s, playing in hundreds of games.

Much has been written about two of the Lancashire lady footballers from this period, Lily Parr (1905–78) and Alice Woods (1899–1991). Alice stopped playing for the then Preston Ladies after marriage in 1928 (her married name was Stanley), but Lily was later inducted into the English Football Hall of Fame.

The ban on ladies' use of FA football pitches was not lifted until 1971.

ATHLETICS

Evidence for amateur athletics can be found in village sports and rural gatherings in times past where running, jumping and throwing events took place. Athletic competition also played an important role in military fitness training in the early 1800s. Later, as the army started to settle into permanent 'home' barracks, military competitions became more fixed and organised. By mid-century the universities at Cambridge and Oxford were organising amateur athletic competitions and the first athletic clubs began to spring up. School sports days followed shortly after.

The first acknowledged national championships were held in 1866 and the first documented running club, the Thames Hare and Hounds, was formed a year later when twelve young male amateur rowers headed for Wimbledon Common and a fitness run of just over 2 miles. In the 1980s the same club had 350 members – male and female. During the mid-Victorian period Mincing Lane Athletics Club (AC) came into existence. Made up mainly from university students, it has come to be regarded as the athletic equivalent of cricket's MCC. Later the club changed its name to London AC.

Sports historians studying this period are happy to write about the 'coming of amateurism', thus acknowledging that amateurism had not been a natural condition in athletics before. Many of the newly formed clubs refused admission to 'manual workers and artisans' on the grounds that they could not 'afford' to be amateurs and belonged to a class that was still producing the bulk of contemporary professional runners. Between the 1860s and '80s the amateur/professional issue was to hamper the formation of a unified national organisation. The eventual formation of the Amateur Athletic Association in 1880 heralded in the era of serious amateur competition and the consequent keeping of written records relating to competitors and their times. Interest in athletics increased as a result of the revival of the Olympic Games and especially after they were held in London for the first time in 1908.

From the outset the national AAA championships rotated between London, the Midlands and the North. The first contest was held at Lillie Bridge in London and the second in Birmingham. Huddersfield and Northampton were also venues on more than one occasion. The 100yds, always a popular event, was dominated by London AC while interesting evidence for multi-sport participation can be seen in the control over the 120yd hurdles held by athletes from the Nottingham Forest FC athletics club. Club members Charles Gowthorpe (born *c.* 1862), an ironmonger's apprentice, and Charles Daft (born 1865), a lace warehouse apprentice in his youth, were both successful in this particular discipline (see the Case Studies chapter for the Daft family).

Field events also began to attract attention. Irish and Scottish competitors proved particularly strong in disciplines associated with this area of the sport and the first pole vault was won by E.A. Strachan of the Royal Inniskilling Fusiliers. Not all the modern events were competed for in the late Victorian period; discus and javelin did not come into play until 1914.

It is also noteworthy that the junior and women's AAA competition did not start until the 1930s.

Both amateur distance running and race walking provide interesting areas of study. They seem to have replaced the professional pedestrianism of the early nineteenth century and professional short and middle distance track racing of the mid-Victorian period in terms of competitive popularity.

Alfred 'Alfie' Shrubb (1879–1964) was one of the most successful distance runners of all time. He was Sussex-born and his family worked on the land. Shrubb himself was a bricklayer and when his running talent was spotted he became a member of the Horsham Blue Star Harriers. He ran as an amateur until 1905 and then as a professional. Running distances, which required about an hour to complete, he eventually captured nearly thirty world records. He died in Canada where an annual race is held in memory of 'The Little Wonder'.

Another Sussex man, policeman George Larner, enjoyed considerable race walking success in the 1908 London Olympics, while William Sturgess proved victorious in a number of AAA walking championships around the turn of the century. Distance races took place between Croydon and Goldstone, Blackpool and Manchester, and London and Brighton. Successful clubs in the field of walking included Belgrave Harriers and the Surrey Walking Club.

Preston in Lancashire provides us with a useful example of the type of development taking place in amateur athletics within an urban environment. Amateur athletics arrived in the town in 1870 with a festival and medals and prizes for 'Flat Racing, Jumping, Pole Leaping, Gymnastics, Boxing, Walking and Cycling'. A gymnastic and athletic club was formed five years later to promote this as an annual event. Thousands turned up and the event continued to take place for the rest of the century. The Preston Harriers were formed in 1881, mainly as a result of this enthusiasm.

Despite an interest in distance running among seasoned athletes, road racing did not become a public sport until the great running boom of the 1970s, which gave birth to hundreds of new running clubs to rival the older ones already in existence. Ancestral amateur athletes can be best followed up via the older clubs and their histories, for example South London and Birchfield. Forty-four such clubs came together with the formation of the AAA and by 1964 over 1,200 also enjoyed membership.

The growth of amateur athletics in the late Victorian period was tied into a more general religious movement that stood opposed to betting and professionalism in sport. The anti-alcohol temperance movement was involved too, its organisers viewing amateur sport as having a sobering and therapeutic influence – one contemporary training manual spoke highly of brine baths and balletic exercises. The introduction of the Whitsun bank holiday in 1871 was a great boost to athletics and Whitsuntide sports across the country attracted thousands of participants. Fertile ground here for family historians in search of sporting ancestors.

BADMINTON

Competitive badminton is a sport belonging to the twentieth century. Created at Badminton Hall in Gloucestershire in the 1860s and known at times as shuttlecock and battledore, it remained a leisure-time pursuit for the remainder of the Victorian period. In fact, badminton was described in one twentieth-century encyclopaedia as a 'disorganised pastime' – and this despite the creation of a set of rules in India in the 1880s.

The move towards organisation of the sport came with the creation of the Badminton Association in 1893, which became the Badminton Association of England in the 1930s when an international association was established. the All England Championships, recognised for many years as the most prestigious in the world, started in 1899. Scotland and Ireland had open championships too, and international badminton started in the 1902/3 season with a match in Dublin between England and Ireland.

The competitive formula of badminton was very similar to that of lawn tennis from the outset, with championships in singles for men and women, men's doubles, women's doubles and mixed doubles. Men's singles champion in 1902 and 1903 was Ralph Watling. The only male of this name to show in appropriate censuses via *The Genealogist* search engine was the son of a Norfolk maltster and corn merchant who was around 30 in 1902. Ethel Warneford Thomson, Islington-born and a doctor's daughter, won eleven All England Championships and was inducted into the Badminton Hall of Fame in 2009. Her badminton career was established in Devon, a place that produced a number of successful players. Henry Marrett, a Streatham-based doctor, was another early badminton champion.

Badminton clubs sprang up across the country in the twentieth century and many of them now have brief histories online. At Clandon in Surrey, an extra round of bricks was added to the new village hall in the 1920s to enable badminton to be played. Hull Badminton Club, founded in 1912, claims to be the 'oldest purely badminton club in England'.

BASKETBALL

Basketball has been a keenly supported and contested minority sport (both professional and amateur) in Britain from the latter part of the twentieth century. Despite its popularity in the United States in the beginning of that century and an early demonstration of the sport in London in the 1890s, it did not really establish roots in Britain until the 1930s. International games were then played and teams began to spring up, especially among the armed forces. The sport proved particularly popular with youth organisations like the YMCA. It is as members of such organisations that ancestral basketball players are likely to have enjoyed competition, with London Central YMCA becoming a breeding place for future internationals. Other successful clubs in this period included Catfield Saints, Hoylake YMCA and Rochdale Greys.

BILLIARDS

Until overtaken by snooker in the middle of the twentieth century, professional billiards was a highly competitive sport. Amateur billiards had its day too and billiards was popular both as pastime and sport throughout the nineteenth century. Burleigh House in Lincolnshire, for example, has an excellent billiard room and table dating back to the time of the Napoleonic Wars. The English Amateur Championships were held from the 1880s and world championships from 1926. Welsh, Scottish and women's championships came into play during the mid-twentieth century.

The first English national competition attracted forty-four entries and had qualifying rounds, in which players from northern England were considered to be those living north of Warwickshire and also included competitors from Ireland. A Scottish area qualification was set up at Dumfries for the country's two entries. The final was held in Manchester. Among key players in Victorian times were A.P. Gaskell of London and W.D. Courtenay. Gaskell won the championship five times in a row and Courtenay followed him with two consecutive successes. Arthur Wisdom of Southsea was another important player.

The English Amateur Billiards Association is still going strong and has a deep sense of its history.

BOAT RACING OR AQUATICS

Amateur boat racing has a history as lengthy and full as its professional counterpart. The oldest surviving club, Leander, was established soon after the end of the Napoleonic Wars and there is also evidence for rowing clubs in earlier times. The first boat race between Oxford and Cambridge took place in 1829, although this was not over what is the now traditional course. The history of this race is well covered by books and on websites, with details of the rowers easy to pick up.

The Blue Riband of amateur boat racing was the Diamond Sculls, which began in 1844 and, like many of the top amateur rowing competitions, was dominated by rowers from the universities and the top clubs in its early days. Another important race was the Wingfield Sculls, which was effectively the amateur single sculling championship of the Thames. First competed for in the 1830s, it was open to amateurs from Great Britain and Northern Ireland and was rowed over various courses along the river during the nineteenth century.

Two rowers successful in both these events were Alexander Casamajor (1833–61) and Alfred Dicker (1852–1938). Casamajor won the Wingfield Sculls in six successive years, as well as the Diamond Sculls. His early death came as the result of a ruptured blood vessel. Dicker was a clergyman who won the Wingfield Sculls twice and the Diamond Sculls three times. London-born, he was the vicar of Newchurch on the Isle of Wight at the time of the 1891 census.

The eight-oared Grand Challenge Cup was first rowed for in 1839 at Henley, with the four-oared Stewards Cup beginning two years later. The latter was coxed until 1873. The paired Silver Goblets and Nickalls Challenge Trophy dates from 1845. This competition has a rather lengthy name because it started life with a pair of silver wherries as the prize. This changed to a pair of goblets in 1850 and to the Challenge Cup by the end of the nineteenth century. As with similar competitions it was mainly university and top club rowers who enjoyed success.

Named individuals were also responsible for important technical developments in the sport. The first outrigger sculling boat was developed in the 1840s by two Cambridge undergraduates – Frederick Furnivall (1825–1910) of Trinity Hall and John Beesley of St John's College – and was used by the Cambridge eight in 1845. Furnivall was a remarkable character; he took a maths degree and then went on to be one of the founders of the Oxford English Dictionary. He had a lifelong interest in rowing and promoted it among working-class girls.

Amateur boat racing continued its popularity long after the professional sport had gone into decline and there are many examples of new boat houses being constructed during the Edwardian area. The Royal Chester Rowing Club is a good example of a club with a long history. Founded in 1838, it claims to be the 'oldest rowing club in the United Kingdom'. The emergence of rowing as an Olympic sport in the twentieth century ensured its continued popularity, while the 1908 Olympics in London provided a particular focus.

As with many other sports, the line between amateur and professional often became blurred due to the presence of betting and backing. In 1831, for example, Oxford University and Leander raced each other at Henley for a bet of £200 aside. As with athletics, the establishment of a national amateur rowing organisation took some time due to disputes over attitudes towards professionalism.

BOWLS

Green Bowls is regarded as an English occupation although the sport has very strong roots in Scotland. Sir Francis Drake and the game he 'just had to finish' before facing the Spanish Armada in 1588 must bear much of the blame for the English tag. This noted, bowls had been played in Southampton since the end of the thirteenth century. There was also a professional betting and backing version of the game in the collieries of north-east England (see The Professionals chapter). Places such as Birmingham had numerous bowling greens in the seventeenth and eighteenth centuries but these became neglected as bowls went into decline in the early nineteenth century. North of the border it was a different story; bowls continued to flourish and Scotland had hundreds of clubs by the 1850s. The sport's popularity was strengthened when a Glasgow solicitor laid down a set of rules in 1849.

In England, a revival of interest in bowls came in the late Victorian period. Many new clubs were formed and the sport was a great favourite of the legendary cricketer W.G. Grace, who competed at the highest level. However, English bowls did not really become organised until Edwardian times with the formation of the English Bowling Association (EBA) in 1903. The Scottish national organisation had already been around for a decade by then. Much of this organisation came as part of an effort to ensure that the game remained an amateur one and did not fall into the hands of betters and backers.

In 1904 there were fewer than fifty bowls clubs in England, but by the late 1950s there were almost 2,500, so it is hardly surprising that many families boast a 'bowler' in their ancestry. Over the years it came to be regarded as a sport for older folk – or certainly for older, middle-class men with time on their hands. It proved particularly attractive to those with 'a good eye' who had succeeded in more active sports when young. Moves to include women bowlers came at quite a late stage.

In the early years of EBA competition the far north was at the fore. The first men's singles champion, however, was J.G. Carruthers of the Muswell Hill Club in London, who defeated J. Telford of Newcastle West End. The next champion was Charles Cummings from Sunderland Bowling Club (of which the author is a current member). In the following eight years, four winners came from the far north of England while the first two fours competitions were won by rinks from Carlisle clubs. International competition followed soon after. All four home nations were playing games in Edwardian times and inter-county matches commenced in England in 1911. Middlesex and Surrey took the bowls laurels away from the north and the game continued to grow in the south. By mid-century the former county had 240 competitive bowls clubs and the latter 245.

Crown Green Bowling (where the green peaks to a crown in the centre and falls away to the sides) took a hold in certain parts of the country. In Lancashire and Staffordshire, for example, this form of the sport grew alongside the more traditional form of the game. The British Crown Green Association was set up in 1907 and its first championships held in 1908. Five of the first nine county championships went to Lancashire.

According to a well-researched 1950s encyclopaedia of sport, the combined sports of bowling 'exceeded any other sport' in terms of numbers of participants.

BOXING

Prizefighting involved large sums of money and was such a 'rags to riches' sport that it is hardly surprising to find boxers with talent entering the professional ranks in times past. For most of the nineteenth century what amateur boxing there was took place in the armed forces, where the sport was seen as a good way of keeping fit. With competitions taking place in the army at company, battalion and regimental level, boxing also carried with it a great deal of pride. References to boxing bouts often turn up in diaries and letters belonging to soldiers involved in the two major conflicts of the twentieth century. Equally, those involved in national service at a later date discovered that a talent for boxing could lead to a relatively cosy passage through their brief career in the forces (this applied to all branches of the armed services).

The Amateur Boxing Association (ABA) was established in 1880 and can be seen as part of the movement which grew up in opposition to betting and professionalism in sport around that time. Gloves became an essential part of the sport (although, as noted in the chapter on professional boxing, the idea of using gloves was not entirely new). Other major differences between the amateur and professional sport include the number of rounds per fight (usually three in amateur boxing instead of up to twelve or fifteen in the professional game) plus the use of head guards by amateurs.

Successful amateur boxers came from all walks of life and the sport also benefited from becoming an Olympic sport from the relatively early years of the modern Olympics. There were fights at the 1904 Olympics held in St Louis but they were dominated by Americans. Four years later when Lady Luck brought the Olympics to London as a result of a volcanic eruption in Italy, most of the boxing contestants (and, therefore, most of the champions) were British (see the Olympic section of the chapter).

As with the professional game, the first 'weighted' bouts and championships took place at heavyweight, middleweight and lightweight. In the case of amateur boxing, these were fought in 1881 soon after the formation of the ABA. Early success at heavyweight was enjoyed by H. Dearsley, who boxed for both the Thames and St James clubs, at middleweight by A. Curnick of the Clapton and West London ABCs, and at lightweight by E. Dettmer of the Stanhope ABC. Other influential early clubs include Polytechnic ABC, Belsize ABC, Middleton ABC and Goldsmith Institute ABC. Geoff Townsend of Goldsmiths succeeded at both middleweight and heavyweight in the 1890s.

Amateur boxing clubs have always been at the root of the sport and this is where most ancestral boxers are likely to be found. London had many such clubs in the twentieth century with Manchester, Cardiff and Edinburgh also enjoying championship success alongside representatives of the armed forces. London's Lynn AC Boxing Club has a continuous history from 1892 and provided ABA champions in the nineteenth century, as well as an outstanding professional in Danny Williams in the late twentieth century.

As a footnote, it cannot escape notice that the amateur boxing champions seem to have enjoyed lengthier and happier lives than many of their professional counterparts!

CRICKET

Unwaged cricketers who played at the top level of the game were defined as gentleman amateurs, though in terms of ancestral playing of the game for fun, this group was a relatively small one. As with association football, many British male ancestors (and English ones in particular) will have been asked to play cricket at some point in their lives. If this ended in a representative match for a school, university, club, county or even country, there is every chance that some form of record was kept and may have survived. It is more likely that a cricketing ancestor will have played for fun rather than for money – although, as noted in the section on professionalism, the lines between amateur and professional can at times be blurred. The expenses of a top amateur were often extreme, with a single bottle of expensive champagne and a couple of Cuban cigars going a long way towards eclipsing the wages earned by the hard-toiling pros.

Competitive cricket was firmly established in one form or another by the 1840s. A form well recorded in terms of amateur input is that which

preceded the start of first-class cricket in the 1860s, when teams of professionals were touring the country playing against the odds. The odds, usually
twenty or twenty-two in number, were made up mostly of local club cricketers, sportsmen and dignitaries looking to have their names in lights. This
side would also contain one or two professional ringers. As these games
brought some of the best known professionals in the land to the area, they
were usually well supported by local citizens and thoroughly covered in
the local newspaper. If your ancestor was a well-known amateur sportsman – and especially a cricketer – in the 1840s and '50s, this may well be
worth chasing up. Some of the later games of this type were also caught by
photography in its infancy and remain amongst the most valued of early
sporting photographs.

Where amateurs played first-class cricket after 1864, their stories and
biographies appear alongside those of the professionals and even the least
successful of amateurs gains a reference. The *Cricketers' Who's Who*, for
example, mentions amateur William Ilbert Hancock (1873–1910), who was
born in Somerset, attended Dulwich School and made a single appearance
for Somerset in 1892, amassing a mere seven runs in two innings. He died in
Marylebone in 1910. At the other end of the range is The Right Honourable
Frank Stanley Jackson (1870–1947). Known as 'F.S.', he attended Harrow and
Cambridge, played 200 games for Yorkshire and twenty tests for England.
He was a successful captain of his country, fought in the Boer War, became
an MP and later the Governor of Bengal. He died in London at the Hyde
Park Hotel, Knightsbridge.

The first-class gentleman amateur may have played in the same side as
the professional player but there was always a division between the two.
Gentlemen were usually accorded their initials when their names appeared
in the press or on scorecards. Professionals were referred to by surname
alone, though later they were allowed their initials behind their surname.
There was an annual match, keenly contested, between gentlemen and players. This was first played in the early nineteenth century and continued until
well within living memory. It has also been noted that amateurs tended
to be batsmen rather than bowlers and were often more flamboyant and
adventurous in their play than their professional counterparts – for them,
failure would be less costly!

The majority of amateur cricketers learnt their cricket at school and, in
many cases, followed the game up at university. A survey of 234 Oxford and
Cambridge cricketing 'blues' awarded between 1827 and 1854 reveals that

140 of them attended Eton, Harrow or Winchester. Rugby, Westminster, Tonbridge and Charterhouse were other schools with good reputations for the sport. Generally, cricket was played with great enthusiasm in public schools and urban grammar schools. Match reports and results were published in the termly school magazines. Records of matches between Oxford and Cambridge exist from 1827 and these two institutions tended to dominate university cricket (although Durham University also became a good breeding ground for cricketers in the twentieth century).

Two good examples of amateurs within this system are Alfred James Lowth (1817–1907) and Reginald Hankey (1832–86). Lowth (nicknamed Dandy) attended both Harrow and Winchester and so impressed that he was invited to play in the gentlemen and players match though still a schoolboy. He took nine wickets. Only 5ft 4in, he was described as a 'Pocket Hercules' and was acknowledged as a beautiful bowler. Hankey was born in London, died in Sussex and was 'one of the best batsmen in the land', enjoying enormous success at Harrow School and Oxford University. His brief biography in the *Cricketers' Who's Who* notes 'business restricted his appearances in important cricket'. Unmarried, he was living in London with his sister and servants as a retired banker at the time of the 1881 census.

Club cricket was well established in many areas by the Victorian period, with some clubs retaining detailed records back to the very early nineteenth century – Castle Cary in Somerset and Bishopwearmouth and Stockton in County Durham are good examples of such clubs (see How to Research Sporting Ancestors). In Lancashire, Manchester Cricket Club was an early focal centre for cricket. Formed in 1816, it played games against other teams from the north of England, with a series of matches against the Sheffield side in the 1840s and '50s now regarded as laying the foundation for future Lancashire/Yorkshire battles.

By the end of the nineteenth century cricket leagues were in full swing with those in Lancashire and Yorkshire predominant. From 1895 there was also a Minor Counties Championship with the county sides made up mostly from amateurs. Norfolk, Durham and Worcestershire enjoyed early success here (the latter two are now first-class counties). Most of the minor counties have written records and histories.

The vast majority of amateur ancestral cricketers will have played their cricket as members of one of the Church or Sunday league sides which sprang up in towns and cities or as part of one of the older village cricket sides. The urban leagues were enormously popular from Edwardian times onwards and results and match details were often reported in the local press. The same applies to village cricket where surprising records still turn up in old newspapers and the cupboards of ancient pavilions.

An anonymous writer nicknamed 'The Gaffer' posted a wonderful description of a typical Edwardian village match in an edition of *The Cricketer and Hockey Player* magazine of 1907. One of the teams was his own village side, based in the Severn Valley in Shropshire. Hedges, thistles and brambles, all havens for lost balls, surrounded the ground. The squire's daughter did the scoring and a small boy looked after the scoreboard. The grey-haired squire captained the side, wearing his MCC cap. He bowled to a large coal miner who opened for the opposition; they looked 'a strange pair'. Behind the stumps was the bad-tempered village postmaster, while the close fielder had only one arm.

Games like this could be found the length and breadth of the country – and not only in Edwardian times.

CROQUET

Although seen by many participants as a pastime rather than a sport, croquet enjoyed considerable popularity at certain points during Victorian and Edwardian times. Many heated matches played on the front lawns of country houses will have gone unrecorded, but for other players it was a competitive sport and records have survived. In the late nineteenth century it came to be closely linked with lawn tennis, a sport which took over from croquet in terms of popularity during the 1880s. As with tennis, croquet had an appeal for both sexes.

Croquet competitions took place at Wimbledon and Hurlingham in the late 1860s and early '70s, with textbooks about the sport published during the same period. There is something of a dispute as to who was the first national croquet champion, with some writers taking up the cause of Walter Jones-Whitmore, who won a competition at Evesham in 1867. Walter Peel, a major player in the game, was another claimant. The All England Croquet Club was founded at Wimbledon in 1869. Among the successful ladies a Miss Joad was champion in 1869 and Miss K. Philbrick victor in 1876, 1877, 1881 and 1882. Despite her success at national level, Miss Philbrick is hard to track down (see the Case Studies chapter). Nora J. Beausire, ladies champion in 1909, was in her early 20s when she won the championship. Born in Birkenhead in 1886, she was the daughter of a Lancashire-born businessman trading with South America.

After giving way to lawn tennis in the 1880s, croquet enjoyed a revival of interest in the '90s. It once again had its own separate association and mixed doubles came into vogue by the end of the century. This popularity continued up to the outbreak of the First World War, when the association had 170 affiliated clubs. Cheltenham, with its strong links to the sport, remains as the headquarters for the Croquet Association today.

CURLING

Curling became organised in Scotland from the 1830s and received royal patronage. What was to become the Royal Caledonian Curling Club was set up in 1838 and, by the 1880s, it was so well established that a history of the first fifty years of the club was requested and subsequently written up. Produced by a minister of the church, John Kerr, this was published in 1890 and can now be seen online in its entirety. From Kerr's work it is clear that curling had a developmental period in the early nineteenth century and subsequently took off with the growth of the Royal Caledonian club.

By the end of the nineteenth century every parish in Scotland was said to have facilities for the sport. Curling, like golf, also enjoyed support from exiled Scots and outdoor rinks were to be found in major cities such as Birmingham and Manchester during the late Victorian period. In 1924 Great Britain's team of eight took the gold in curling at the first Winter Olympics. It included an Irishman, Major D.G. Ashley, who won another medal in the same event while curling for Sweden.

A particularly valuable part of Kerr's work covers the meeting that took place in 1838 to sort out the rules of the game. Forty-four gentlemen were present, who represented thirty-six clubs, 'connected with the various districts of Scotland, from Dumfries to Perth'. These included William Stark, James Gay and James Somerville from Kirknewton, and Charles Cowan, William Gilbert and John Renton from Penicuik. Kerr also wrote an engaging account of a trip to Canada made by Scottish curlers during the early Edwardian period.

Mr Punch cycling in *Punch*, 1866. (Author's collection)

CYCLING

Cycling grew up side by side with amateur athletics in the Victorian period. Its development formed part of the same movement towards Christian 'clean living' and away from the temptation to drink and gamble offered by involvement in bare-knuckle boxing, racing and professional running. The two sports often appeared on the same bill, especially at the Whitsuntide sports meetings that began to spring up in the 1880s and '90s organised by various sporting clubs. Englishman James Moore won a cycle race in Paris as early as 1868 and the sport began to blossom in Britain from 1878 to 1899. In the 1870s, the Molineux Ground at Wolverhampton attracted big crowds for cycling events.

Although cycling was highly competitive from the mid-Victorian period onwards, the 1880s proved a key decade. This was when the pneumatic tyre was patented, giving rise to the safety bicycle and a whole new world of sport. Prior to this invention, races had taken place on bone-shakers and both penny-farthings and tricycles had their racing adherents. Races are recorded as having taken place over 1, 5, 25 and 50 mile courses during this period. Herbert Cortis, a medical student, was outstanding over most distances. He rode an Invincible or penny-farthing, and was the first to record a distance of 20 miles in an hour on a bicycle. Though Yorkshire-born and of Yorkshire stock, he was raised in London where his father was a general practitioner.

Another renowned English cyclist of the day was Frederick T. Bidlake, born in Islington in the 1860s. A tutor and later a London-based author and journalist, Bidlake set a tricycle record of 410 miles in twenty-four hours at Herne Hill Velodrome in 1893. By then tracks had begun to spring up all over the country. Herne Hill had opened in 1891, three years after the one at Paddington, while both the Midlands and north-east England were simply awash with tracks. Despite this, many competitions over shorter distances still took place on grass at athletics meetings. Bidlake died in 1933 as a result of a cycling accident on the roads.

Herbert Synger, amateur champion during the early days of the safety bicycle, was a Nottingham man, born into a lace-making family. As with many Midlands athletes, he did a great deal of his fitness training at the Droitwich Brine Baths. In Wales the Aberdare Workmen's Bicycle Club, formed in 1894, was home to many successful cyclists.

Records were kept from the 1890s onwards and these reveal a penchant for long-distance events: from London to Brighton and back (on tricycles in the early days) and an 870 mile race from Land's End to John O'Groats. Cycling was very popular with women but in the early days this was more as a pastime than a competitive sport. It was also an important part of the Whitsuntide meetings, which began to grow up in the middle to late Victorian period. Evidence is mounting that gate money from these meetings had an important role to play in the financial upkeep of the clubs involved.

FENCING

Fencing developed as a competitive sport in Britain during the latter years of the reign of Victoria and the early years of Edward VII. The Amateur

Fencing Association was formed in 1902 and remained amateur until the closing decade of the twentieth century. Prior to the upsurge in interest much had been written about the art of swordplay and there had been fencing activity, often in the shape of demonstrations. Two of the main people involved here were Alfred Hutton and Egerton Castle. At the time of the 1881 census Castle was at military college; ten years later he was a captain in the Royal Engineers. Unsurprisingly, many who took an interest in swordplay were military or ex-military men.

Competitions in foil and sabre took place at national level from 1898 and an early expert was Captain W. Edgeworth Johnstone, who was captured in one of the famous *Vanity Fair* prints. The Épée was added to competition in 1904 and the ladies' foil in 1907. Fencing was also included in the early modern Olympics. Épée and sabre appeared at all the Summer Olympics, though the foil was missing from the London Games of 1908.

FIVES

Although popular for many years, fives (and especially Eton fives) was enjoyed as a leisure pastime and did not become truly organised until well into the twentieth century. Both public schools and clubs enjoyed competition from the 1920s and '30s.

GOLF

The early story of golf appears in both the amateur or professional chapters. It is clear that money frequently changed hands in early one-on-one contests and competitions, yet the history books tend to talk of professionalism in its true sense as existing only from the early nineteenth century onwards. This makes it safer to refer to what went before as amateur.

It is highly likely that any early golfing ancestor will have had Scottish blood in him, as even the most famous English Club at Royal Blackheath owed its existence to Scottish exiles. Belgium and the Netherlands claim the actual origins of the sport of golf as well as Scotland, though the Scottish claim remains a very good one. There are solid records of golfing activity in the country in the late medieval period with named golfers turning up soon after.

Much of the golf played in the early days took place in central Scotland and, in particular, around Edinburgh, with Leith claiming a real birthright. In the late seventeenth century a shoemaker from the city named John Patersone was a local champion and was able to purchase a house out of one set of winnings. In 1724 a game between nobleman Alexander Elphinstone and John Porteous, a captain of the city guard, was recorded in some detail. Porteous came to a sticky end a few years later: sentenced to hang, he was lynched by a mob before the deed could be carried out.

By the eighteenth century competitions were being recorded and prizes given out. In Scotland, in 1744, surgeon John Rattray (1707–71) won a silver club. Rattray was also a skilled archer. What was to become the Royal and Ancient Golf Club of St Andrews was formed in 1754. At London's Blackheath Golf Club, Henry Foot put up a silver driver, or cleek, as a prize in 1766. Golf, however, remained relatively disorganised without any firm agreement as to the actual number of holes that constituted a golf course. It was not until the nineteenth century that much of the golf played was on a professional basis, although an attempt was made to set up an amateur competition at Prestwick in Scotland in the 1850s. This competition only lasted for two years. The winner on the second occasion was Robert Chambers, compiler of the famous *Chambers Encyclopaedia*. There were very few golf clubs in existence at this time.

The revival of amateur competition came with the establishment of the amateur championship at Hoylake on the Wirral Peninsula in England in 1885. Early victors of the amateur championship included local men Harold Hilton (1869–1942) and John Ball Jnr (1861–1940). Ball won the amateur championship eight times, as well as the Open as an amateur. He was the first English-born golfer to win the Open and was inducted into Golf's Hall of Fame in the 1970s. Hilton won the amateur championship four times and the Open twice. His father was in the assurance business and Hilton himself worked as secretary to a golf clerk according to the 1901 census.

Golf was expanding in England during the late nineteenth century too. After the Royal Blackheath Club (see The Professionals chapter) came the Old Manchester Club and the North Devon at Westward Ho!. Cheap land in the countryside during the agricultural depression of 1880–1914 also allowed new clubs to be established.

The Welsh, Scottish, Irish and Women's amateur championships date from the years after the First World War, as does the Walker Cup. Women's golf has a lengthy history, with the St Andrew's Ladies Golf Club set up in 1867 and followed shortly by other clubs in south-west England. Clubs at Musselburgh, Carnoustie and Wimbledon date back to the early 1870s. By the mid-1890s there were sixteen ladies clubs in Scotland and research has shown that many of their members were from outside the area – simply enjoying a spot of holiday golf. The Ladies Golf Union was established in 1893.

One interesting early lady golfer was born Dorothy Campbell in Edinburgh in 1883. She grew up near North Berwick and is recognised as golf's first international female superstar. She won the British amateur championship in 1909 and 1911, and the US amateur championship in 1909, 1910 and 1924. She moved to Canada in 1910 then, upon marrying, to the USA. She died in 1945. A good illustration of the problem of following up female sporting ancestry: Dorothy Campbell played under several names because of a variety of marriages and divorces. She is sometimes referred to as Dorothy Campbell Hurd Howe and competed, at various times, as Dorothy Hurd, Dorothy Campbell Hurd, Mrs J.V. Hurd, and Dorothy Howe.

HOCKEY

Hockey historians proudly describe their sport as being 'the most purely amateur game played in England'. After referring to various early forms of the game played throughout Britain, they usually get to a style of hockey played at Eton around 1830 as a true starting point for the modern game.

In many ways the story of hockey as we know it follows a similar path to that of rugby and in the same geographical areas. In the 1860s it was considered something of a rough game and was played with a one-handed stick, with its modern club roots being set down in the suburbs of London. Blackheath, famed for its part in the early development of rugby, was an initiating club and much of the early male hockey activity took place in and around London – especially at Richmond and Teddington. Eventually the game moved from rough ground onto cricket pitches when they were available, although different clubs had different rules.

By 1900 there were some 200 male hockey clubs involved in friendly matches and a functioning national association. Two years later the laws of the game were set out and clarified and an association formed for the clubs playing in and around the capital. Between 1895 and 1907 the international home countries fixture list began to take shape. In England divisional matches between north, south, east and west predated these fixtures, and continued to play a valuable role in the English game and formation of the England team. Britain took gold in hockey at the 1920 Olympics.

A couple of interesting early hockey players were Midlander Ezra Horton (1861–1939) and Cyril Wilkinson. (1884–1970). Horton was both an amateur and a professional footballer with West Bromwich Albion before turning his attention to hockey. He played the sport for England while in his 30s. Durham-born Wilkinson, also a competent cricketer, played his hockey for the Hampstead Club and captained the Great Britain side that took gold at the 1920 Olympics.

Hockey was also one of the first ladies' team sports to develop fully. The All England Women's Hockey Association was established in the 1890s soon after the formation of the first private club (the development of an organisation in Ireland was at a still earlier date). Early English clubs were at Molesey, Wimbledon and Ealing. The sport spread like wildfire and took root in schools and especially in the private schools. Prominent among these were Westminster House (later Roedean) and St Leonard's. Hockey also gained popularity in the ladies' colleges at Oxford and Cambridge. At Girton College in the 1890s, the hockey players sang the following to the tune of popular music hall song *Wot Cher*:

Play up, all the college cried
Pass out to the wings, girls
That's the sort of thing, girls
Run! Run! I thought I would have died
Knocked it through the Newnham goal

A number of such songs have survived as fine examples of the sport's popularity. One history devoted to girls' schools suggests that interest grew because hockey replaced a regime of boring gym exercises and brisk walks. In addition, it allowed female participants a period of relief from long skirts and stays. The real development of women's hockey, however, came after the First World War. All-rounder Lottie Dod played international hockey (see Case Studies).

HORSE RACING

If there is an area where the simplistic amateur/professional divide collapses then this is it. It has already been noted that to most 'gentlemen' – even in the early twentieth century – sport was not sport unless there was a quarry at the end of it or a chase for fun. The mid-Victorian editions of *Punch* magazine are filled with cartoons of men and women hunting on horseback, and it was from hunting that the sport known for years as steeplechasing emerged. Its modern title, National Hunt Racing, thus betrays the sport's origins.

Steeplechasing is thought to have originated in Ireland with races taking place between fixed points, which were often church steeples, and across rough terrain covered with fences, hedges and ditches. Those competing were usually 'amateur' huntsmen extending their idea of sport, although wagers and prize money tend to cloud the picture somewhat.

Steeplechasing developed in England in the late eighteenth century and settled into a pattern in the early nineteenth century. There were experiments at Newmarket, St Albans and Aylesbury, with Cheltenham, still famed for its racing over fences, entering the fray in 1835. By 1839 the race now known as The Grand National had started to take shape in Liverpool, though the common name was not attached to the race until 1847. One of the great characters of its early running was Captain Becher after whom the famous brook fence is named. Becher fought in the Napoleonic Wars and helped to set up jump racing at Aintree. A win there was one of many during Captain Becher's distinguished career. He had further success in several of the most prestigious steeplechases, including the Northamptonshire Chase, the Grand Aylesbury Chase, the St Albans Steeplechase and the Cheltenham Steeplechase – an indicator of the spread of the new sport. In the early days many of the riders over fences were military men.

In towns and cities across England racing over jumps became an annual event, backed enthusiastically by local businessmen and by publicans in particular. The majority of these festivals were not long-lasting. Between the 1860s and the '80s this relatively new sport became more organised and the term 'National Hunt' began to be used. A National Hunt champion jockey award system has run in one shape or another since 1900, the prize going to the rider with most victories in a season. Professionals have dominated the award although amateurs H.S. Sydney, Jack Anthony and H. Brown were successful in the early days. Anthony was a Welshman and was inducted into the Welsh Sports Hall of Fame towards the end of the twentieth century.

HURLING AND GAELIC FOOTBALL

Sports associated with Ireland were organised and developed along strictly amateur and hierarchical lines. One of the historians of Irish sport, Mike Cronin, notes that the key in the case of both sports lay in the joint term 'born and lived'. From the 1880s onwards the Catholic parish was the hub of native Irish sport. By the early twentieth century there were some 3,000 clubs operating within the system. For the most talented in either sport, movement from the parish was upwards to county level. There were thirty-two of such counties, with the whole process looked after by the overarching Gaelic Athletic Association.

Although dissimilar at first glance, hurling and Gaelic football have more in common than a mere controlling body, such as the size and nature of the pitch and number of players (fifteen). Hurling is a truly ancient sport and in the eighteenth century the Anglo/Irish gentry would often pitch teams of players against each other. As with many amateur sports, the problem of 'pay for play' has arisen at times and been the cause of bitter discussion. The modern rules of Gaelic football were laid down in the mid-1880s.

A best ever Gaelic football fifteen, drawn up in the millennium from players involved in the game from 1884 onwards, included players from Kerry, Galway, Mayo, Cavan, Meath, Laois, Down and Dublin. The county of Limerick was an important centre during the early years of the organ-ised sport, with the Commercials Club founded by employees of Cannock's drapery store having a say in the setting down of rules and enjoying success in the All Ireland Championships.

It has been noted that these sports grew around the same time as associa-tion football and rugby, and that their separate rules were keenly developed to ensure the Irish kept a national identity. It is only in relatively recent times that Croke Park in Dublin has allowed any other than Gaelic sports to be played on its hallowed turf.

An interesting character in hurling was Edward Barrett from County Kerry, who played at one time for his local side at Ballyduff. He later emi-grated to London where he formed part of the London team that defeated Cork in the final of the 1901 All Ireland Championship. This was London's only win and the side was soundly thrashed by Cork in the 1902 final.

ICE SKATING

Ice skating has a lengthy history as an outdoor social pastime, especially in the seventeenth century when a series of hard winters meant frozen rivers and lakes across Britain. It was during this time that an ice skating club was set up in Edinburgh. Later, in the early nineteenth century, huge crowds turned up to watch and bet upon agricultural labourers speed skating on the Fens. The history of Fenland skating is a story in itself and produced characters as marked as the rowers on the Tyne and the wrestlers in Cumberland and Cornwall (see The Professionals chapter).

A treatise on figure skating was published by Englishman Robert Jones in the 1770s, but it was another century before the sport became truly organised. James Drake Digby founded the National Skating Association in Cambridgeshire in 1879 partly as a result of worry over the increasingly 'professional' nature of the Fenland speed skating. The popularity of the sport increased on the back of the introduction of indoor facilities. The first successful artificial glaciarium appeared in London in the 1870s, enabled by the discovery of artificial refrigeration. Others rinks followed shortly after – at Rusholme in Manchester for example, but the skating there was said to be non-competitive and balletic, and the facility did not stay open for long.

British speed skating championships for men were held from 1880 onwards with a number of participants coming from the Fenland area. These champions included W. Loveday (in 1889–90), A. Aveling (1892) and A. Tebbit (1902–05). The Aveling family is of particular interest. Both James (b. 1869) and Bob Aveling enjoyed success in the amateur field despite their Fenland background (their father was a JP and deputy lieutenant of Cambridgeshire and Huntingdonshire). James competed in Norway and is acknowledged as having much to do with the introduction of the speed skate.

By the end of the Victorian era he had succeeded in the British championships at nearly every distance. International success was hampered by oval courses as in England the courses were straight. Bob was also a British champion. At the time of the 1881 census the two brothers were to be found on their father's farm in March, Cambridgeshire. The household had a cook/dairymaid and two general servants. Figure skating gained in popularity in the late Victorian period and championships developed here too. British skaters did well in international competition with female skater Madge Syres particularly successful in Edwardian times (see the Case Studies chapter). The competition was held as mixed until 1927, when it became male.

LACROSSE

Lacrosse is another sport to be added to the relatively short list of sports enjoyed by both males and females in the Victorian and Edwardian periods. Despite its origins in the lands of the native Americans, lacrosse has been popular in certain schools across the United Kingdom for some time and boasts the admission of a twentieth-century Englishwoman to the Lacrosse Hall of Fame in Baltimore, Maryland.

The playing of lacrosse has tended to been restricted to certain geographical areas in Britain – mainly in and around London, Glasgow and the Lancashire cities of Manchester and Liverpool. The first British club was set up in Glasgow in 1867 and by the end of the century there was considerable competition at both regional and international level. Lacrosse also developed in Ireland.

From the 1870s there were regular contests between north and south in England, with the Iroquois Cup keenly contested at club level. In the north of England the clubs based in Stockport, Liverpool and south Manchester tended to dominate in Victorian times. Further south there were a number of successful clubs including London, Clapton, Surbiton, Snaresbrook, Woodford and Leys School.

POLO

For many years the British have played polo with great enthusiasm both on the Indian subcontinent and at home. Its participants in the early days were mostly army men, though not exclusively from the cavalry despite the equestrian nature of the sport.

Polo developed in India in the late 1850s and the British forces there were engaged in polo competitions from the 1870s, with men from the ninth Lancers, King's Own Scottish Borderers and the first Duke of Wellington's regiments enjoying early success. An inter-regimental trophy was played for from these times, followed by Indian cavalry and infantry trophies in the 1880s and a Subalterns Cup by the turn of the century.

The first recorded game in England was on Hounslow Heath in 1869, between the tenth Hussars and the ninth Lancers. Competitive polo took place at Hurlingham from the 1870s in the shape of the Champions' Cup and another inter-regimental cup. The Subalterns Cup started at Ranelagh in the 1890s. The ninth Hussars showed prowess in England, as did the seventh Hussars and Royal Horse Guards. Competition was abandoned during the early years of Edward's reign because of the Boer War.

Polo remained a fairly popular sport among certain classes in Britain up to the Second World War. Here, one of its main features was a contest between Great Britain and the USA for the Westchester Cup, which was initiated in 1886. Walter Selby Buckmaster (1872–1942) was Wimbledon-born, lived in Brixworth, Northamptonshire and played polo for Great Britain in the early modern Olympics. He worked as a stockbroker. International polo player Frederick Freake was the Hampshire-born son of a vicar who later moved to Gloucester. He won two silver medals in 1900 and 1908 and later became high sheriff of Warwickshire.

ROLLER SKATING AND ROLLER HOCKEY

Roller skates came across from the USA in the 1860s and though roller skating is enjoying something of a revival – in the USA in particular – the influence of roller hockey and roller skating on British society has been neither lengthy nor extensive. Regarded as a pastime rather than a sport, roller skating was something of a fad during Victorian times although it enjoyed a competitive upsurge in Britain during the inter-war years.

Speed records for roller skating were noted down from the 1890s and competitions for men started just before the First World War, with women's just after. The rules for roller hockey were laid down at about the same time. Competitions for figure skating and dancing on roller skates developed around the same period, with the Alexandra Palace and Holland Park, both in London, being popular venues.

The BBC Studios on Delaware Road, Maida Vale, started life as a roller skating palace in 1909 and here Walter Stanton won the first national figure skating title in 1910. Stanton dominated the sport in the years leading up to the First World War. Another important character was Billy Wetherall, the 'World's Champion Endurance Skater'. He was wont to skate for days on end, taking his meals while in motion. This he did around the country, charging a fee to watch that probably qualifies him for the chapter on professionals.

For more on roller skating and roller hockey see the photographic section of sources, where there is a reference to an interesting collection of pictures relating to the sport. One photograph listed is of the England Roller hockey team at Herne Bay, *c.* 1930, with the names of R.R. Hoile, C. Moon, G. Mapley, F. Barling and E. Brown (president of Roller Hockey Association) listed below it.

RUGBY

Rugby was an amateur sport from its foundation (disputably by William Webb Ellis in 1823) until the split into Rugby Union and Rugby League in the late nineteenth century. Rugby Union was to remain, on the surface at least, fiercely amateur for another hundred years, while Rugby League developed a strong amateur game amongst junior clubs in the north of England.

Up to the 1860s rugby and football were also as one (see the Introduction and The Professionals chapter), with the game played mostly at public schools – where what rules there were differed from school to school. Games were organised by the boys themselves and the rules not really formulated until the 1840s. Ancestral involvement in such games may appear in old school records.

In the 1860s came another famous split, between the dribbling game and the carrying game. By then clubs were in existence and the representatives of London's Blackheath turned their backs on the dribbling game, thus becoming the first of the 'modern' rugby football clubs (one of the issues was over 'hacking', which ironically failed to take root in either form of the game and was soon outlawed).

In 1871 twenty-two rugby clubs gathered at a meeting to form a union – Blackheath and Richmond among them (though apparently the Wasps' representative got lost on his way to the meeting). In the years that followed clubs sprang up all over the country and many that were formed in the 1870s and '80s are still playing today. The public school element remained strong in this sport and many of the early participants came from the upper reaches of society, with cricket and rugby going hand in hand as ideal summer and winter sports.

A good example of an early rugby club can be found in Worcester RFC. It began in 1876 and one of its founders and early players was the famous amateur and professional runner Walter George, who was an apprentice at the time. Typical of Victorian sport, the club later expanded to embrace both cycling and athletics. In recent years Worcester has developed into one of England's leading professional Rugby Union clubs. Another good example is Clifton RFC, formed slightly earlier – a club whose history is told on an excellent website and book (see Case Studies). Wakefield Trinity, later to become a league club, started life, as the name suggests, as a Church side.

As with association football, there was no league structure and games consisted of friendlies and knockout cups, many of which were at county level. The Hospitals Cup was played for from 1875, the Yorkshire Cup from 1877 and the Durham Cup from 1881. Internationals then cemented the growing importance of rugby with the Home Nations competition, roughly in place by the 1880s. With one or two exceptions, this remained the structure of Rugby Union until well into the second half of the twentieth century, when both leagues and professionalism entered the game.

Like cricket, rugby was a proud sport and tended to keep records. Local newspapers kept reports on most important local cup games and derbies, photographs were hung on the clubhouse walls and minutes (including team selections) kept in minute books. By the end of the century many of the clubs were running more than one team. Pride was also important in this sport and Swansea's W.J. 'Billy' Bancroft has been credited with initiating much of the passion associated with Wales and rugby. Bancroft represented his country on more than thirty occasions in the late Victorian period. He had all the skills required for the game, which he played both 'mentally' and 'physically'.

The laws of Rugby Union developed slowly. The term 'try' given to the putting the ball with downward pressure behind the goal line is an interesting one. Now a valuable asset in terms of points scored, at first it was worth nothing more than giving the scoring side a 'try' at kicking the ball between the posts. If the kick was successful then a successful plus was gained. Points only came to be awarded in the late nineteenth century.

For researchers looking for ancestral 'footballers' in the north of England it is important to realise that many Rugby League sides existed for twenty or thirty years before the 1890s split as 'ordinary' rugby sides. In many cases they were among the most successful, attracting large crowds and, in contrast to other sides, made up of players from the working class.

Yorkshire clubs such as Leeds, Wakefield Trinity, Dewsbury, Hull and Halifax packed out the grounds for cup matches. Yorkshireman Dickie Lockwood from Heckmondwike was the England captain, while Broughton

Mr Punch likes the new canoeing fad in *Punch's* frontispiece, 3 July 1869. (Author's collection)

Rangers, now defunct but significant at the time, imported two Welsh play-ers: the James brothers, David and Evan. Lockwood (1867–1915) was born at Crigglestone and has an interesting 'crossover' history. He played rugby for Dewsbury, Heckmondwike and Wakefield Trinity. At the first club he was a rugby player, at the second he became a Rugby League player, and at the last purely a league player. He captained the England side before the split and at the age of 34 was living in Wakefield, described as a 'wire temperer'.

Of sides, which existed as rugby sides before the split, some moved to Rugby League and subsequently ceased to play; Broughton Rangers, Brighouse Rangers, Heckmondwike and Liversedge may be of particular interest here. Brighouse, which ceased to play professional Rugby League in Edwardian times, still exists as an amateur side. Broughton existed until the Second World War then enjoyed a brief later life as Belle Vue Rangers. Heckmondwike produced other pre-split internationals: Donald Jowett (six caps) and Willie Sutcliffe. Liversedge's Harry Varley and Bob Wood won pre-split England caps, although the Rugby League side folded in 1902. Jowett (1866–1908) was publican of the Crown Hotel, Liversedge, in 1901, having been a brewer's traveller ten years earlier when he lived at home in his mother's grocery shop. The pressure to succeed and improve came on those clubs with the largest support, and it is perhaps natural that the northern clubs should move to professionalism. As in the case of association football, it was, in the end, merely accepting what was already in existence.

Rugby Union's legendary strength in Wales is to be seen from early times with Aberavon, Cardiff and Llanelli operational in the 1890s. The Welsh also took kindly to the idea of leagues with the formation of the Glamorgan and the Monmouth. Here, the story of Ferndale RFC makes for particularly interesting reading. Formed in the early 1880s, the side entered the league system in the 1890s and enjoyed cup-winning success in the years prior to the First World War, attracting crowds of up to 3,000. However, local interest turned to football after the war and the side folded in 1921. Other local sides continued to play until the Second World War, when they too folded. The original club was revived in the late 1980s.

Rugby League also developed an amateur game, although this had been dwindling until an amateur British league system was formed in the 1970s. Amateur rugby has always enjoyed popularity in the heartland of rugby: Yorkshire and Lancashire (including the old Furness area), and also in Cumbria.

SAILING/YACHTING

These two terms seem interchangeable and it is difficult at times, particularly in the early years, to decide whether the sport was amateur or professional as a great deal of money often changed hands. This was true in Stuart times when royalty and nobility enjoyed one-on-one racing for wagers. For the vast majority during the nineteenth century, when the sport really enjoyed popularity, it was simply about the competition.

After the great interest shown in sailing by Charles II in the late seventeenth century the sport went into decline – only to be revived by the Duke of Cumberland, among others, almost a century later. The first yacht club is associated with him and a 'marine fete' was held at Starcross in Devon in the 1770s. In 1780 a regatta took place on Bassenthwaite in the northern part of the English Lake District. The Royal Yacht Club came into being in the early nineteenth century and the famous Cowes Week, based on the Isle of Wight, got under way in the 1820s.

The opening up of inland waters to competitive sailing was an important move and the English Lake District was to have a leading role in the history of the sport. Prominent here was the Windermere (later Royal Windermere) Sailing Club. There was competitive sailing on the lake from the early nineteenth century and the club was formed in the 1860s. It gained its royal warrant in 1887 and opened its first boathouse two years later. The opening up of the railway in the 1840s also had a significant effect and allowed those who could afford it to watch yachting events and regattas and all associated with the popular ferry sports. The Thames Sailing club of Surbiton was formed in 1870.

The Yacht Racing Association was set up in 1875, one of its purposes being to sort out the problems of competition between vessels of different sizes and to introduce fair competition. Sailing appeared in the early Olympics, and around the same time small boat dinghy racing also came into its element under the auspices of the Royal Canoe Club. Warington Baden Powell (1847–1921), the older brother of the founder of the boy scout movement, enjoyed success in dinghy sailing in various versions of the self-built Nautilus during the 1870s and '80s and was also heavily involved with the Royal Canoe Club. Alaric and Edward Tredwen were two other influential small boat sailors (Cornish-born, they were both based in London).

Sailing often involved large crews and benefited from being part of the 1908 London Olympics where there were many British entrants (see the Olympics section at the end of this chapter).

SHOOTING (RIFLE AND SMALL BORE)

As with polo, shooting was a sport with strong military connections. Competitive rifle shooting is strongly linked to the rise of the volunteer movement in the 1860s. This in turn was linked to the perceived threat of invasion by Napoleon III, Emperor of France and nephew of Napoleon Bonaparte. What began simply as necessary training turned rapidly into a sport that appealed to soldiers, both full and part time.

Rifle shooting took place mainly where the military gathered for exercises, initially on Wimbledon Common and later at Bisley Camp. The much coveted Queen's/King's Prize (title decided by the sex of the current reigning monarch) was contested from 1860 and the 'Albert' from 1862 – the year of the prince consort's death. The latter prize was for match rifles. By the out-break of the Boer War teams were also competing for prizes using revolvers.

Competitors in these contests were almost exclusively male, although there was a female winner of the King's Prize in 1930. Schools were also encouraged to develop rifle shooting with the introduction of the Ashburton Challenge Shield from 1861.

The small bore rifle was considered more of a defensive weapon than an attack one, but its use came to be encouraged through competitions developed in the early years of the twentieth century. Field Marshal Earl Roberts was a particular advocate of this sport.

Show Jumping

Sites dedicated to show jumping acknowledge that this is a relatively new sport, only taking off in the twentieth century. Prior to this, much of the related fun and sport took place over distance and in the open, which did not make for much in the way of spectator sport. Although the Dublin Horse Show of 1869 has been recognised as an early sign of sporting possibilities, it was not until 1907 and the Horse of the Year Show that show jumping became effective. Most of the entries here were military personnel. Five years later, show jumping became an Olympic sport. Paul Kenna, Bryan Lawrence, Edward Radcliffe Nash and Edward Scott were well-known early show jumpers, competing in three-day events.

Squash and Racquets

Such is the modern interest in lawn tennis and its history that the historical importance of racquets and the chances of ancestral involvement are often overlooked. Here too was a sport where, unlike others, amateurs and professionals often competed against one another.

Racquets was played mainly in the public schools and at Oxford and Cambridge Universities. From these places it moved into Queen's Club, London and also appeared in a number of naval bases. Competition in the sport is recorded from at least the early nineteenth century, with the jewel in the crown being the Public Schools Championship. This was one of the highlights of the Victorian sporting calendar. Each school was allowed to enter two pairs and there was great internal school rivalry to be made one of the chosen. Between 1868 and 1886 these championships were held at the old Princes Club in London. They were moved briefly to Lord's before settling at the Queen's Club. The championships were competed for in front of packed galleries, with Rugby, Harrow and Eton enjoying early success.

With the existence of school magazines and Corinthian school pride, it is hardly surprising to find the deeds of successful racquet players well recorded. Cuthbert Ottoway (1850–78) was born in Dover and attended Eton and Oxford. He was an outstanding sportsman who captained England's first football team, appeared in FA Cup finals and also played top-level cricket. He was regarded as the 'best amateur racquets player of his day'. He died of TB – not an uncommon end for young Victorian sports-men. George Allan Webbe (1854–1925) was a London-born Harrovian who, with his partner, won the championship in 1871 and 1872. He and two of his brothers were also good cricketers and their father was a fund holder. The Foster family, who are featured in the Case Studies chapter, counted racquets among their sports too. By the end of Victoria's reign, racquets had come a long way from its roots in the debtors' prisons.

A number of reasons are given for the birth of squash or squash racquets, including one which suggests that the sport started life as a form of baby racquets played by young boys on small courts. As noted in the introduc-tion, the modern game of squash enjoyed a major revival in the latter part of the twentieth century, but it had already seen something of a following earlier on. By 1930 there were amateur championships for men and women as well as an open championship. One of the key figures in the early squash movement was Jimmy (Parker) Tomkinson. Playing out of the Squash club in Bath, Tomkinson was already an established racquets player having played the game successfully at Eton. He won the amateur championship at the age of 40 and worked hard to establish rules and structure for the sport up till his death.

Real tennis re-emerged as a sport for the wealthy minority during the late nineteenth century and a number of the courts built then remain in use today. These are cherished for their architectural features.

SWIMMING

Swimming is yet another sport that blossomed in the urban environment of late Victorian Britain. This was despite the creation of public bathing facilities at a much earlier date by an Act of Parliament. In the early days of competition shorter events took place 'in the pool', with distance events established in open water – rivers, lakes and even the sea. At the Olympic Games of 1900 in Paris, swimming events (including an obstacle race) took place in the Seine.

At first all events were freestyle, with one race over a mile taking place in the Thames in 1869. The sport was then given a great boost by Captain Webb's achievement in swimming the Channel in 1875. Between the late 1870s and mid-1880s contests over 100, 220 and 440yds, as well as half a mile, came into being. It is hardly surprising to find these early British sporting distances based on more traditional divisions of the mile, although they have now been replaced by metric distances. This was the case with horse racing, cricket and athletics too, as agricultural usage entered sport. A furlong of 220yds was originally the 'furrow long' expected of an experienced plough-man, and the twenty-two yard chain, used in road and land measurement, was decreed a suitable length for the cricket pitch.

Portsmouth Swimming Club was among the early pioneers of competi-tive swimming and clubs in Leicester and Manchester proved very strong. Races also took place between members of the House of Commons and members of the House of Lords from the 1870s. At one time these were on the Serpentine. Diving from various boards was introduced in Edwardian times. In Scotland the men's Amateur Swimming Association (ASA) cham-pionships started in 1888 and the women's in 1907. After various other organisations in England, the ASA was established in the 1880s.

Swimming was a sport taken up by women and Olympic swimmer Jennie Fletcher dominated domestic competition in the 100yds during the early years of the twentieth century (she was champion in 1901, from 1906–09, and in 1912). John (Jack) Jarvis, a Leicester-born Olympian, won over twenty ASA titles in late Victorian and Edwardian times. Backstroke and breaststroke entered competition in the early twentieth century.

Competitive swimming attracted sportsmen and women from all walks of life and was particularly popular with the working class. This can be seen in the case of a number of those who enjoyed success in river and pool during the early modern Olympic Games.

TABLE TENNIS

More of a pastime as 'ping pong' in the early twentieth century, it did not take off as a sport until the years after the First World War. Men's and women's opens developed then and there was particular enthusiasm for the sport in Wales. The Table Tennis Association was formed in 1922.

TENNIS

Tennis (lawn, hard court and indoor) developed as a professional sport during the second half of the twentieth century. Prior to this amateurs played the game, and especially lawn tennis, at club and competitive level from late Victorian times. Tennis, using its generic term, has a long and complex history and it is clear that the rather strange system of scoring used in lawn tennis today developed at a very early stage. By the end of the eighteenth century interest in the indoor game seems to have tailed off.

The men's game was the first to develop, in the wake of the experiment with sphairistike (or 'sticky' as it was more commonly known) and on the back of some disillusionment with croquet. It soon grew into lawn tennis and Leamington Lawn Tennis Club was named as such in 1874. The All England Croquet and Lawn Tennis Club (1876) introduced its singles competition in 1877. There were twenty-two entries and the winner was Spencer Gore (1850–1906). Gore was Wimbledon-born and bred (though he died in Ramsgate) and was also a good cricketer, succeeding at club level and playing for Surrey on a couple of occasions. He worked as crown receiver and surveyor and at the time of the 1881 census lived in Epsom with his family and a number of servants.

The men's doubles championship followed shortly but up to 1883 these were held at Oxford. At first the sport was dominated by those already familiar with other racket sports and it is now acknowledged that the first to 'grow up in the game' were the Renshaw twins, Willie (1861–1904) and Ernest (1861–99). Willie was the expert singles player, winning the Wimbledon singles title on seven occasions – three of which were against his own brother. The brothers were successful as a doubles partnership, too, and are credited with promoting the 'smash' as an important element in the game. The twins hailed from Leamington Spa and Willie served as a lieutenant in the militia in the 1880s.

The first Wimbledon ladies singles final took place in 1884, but there had been significant competition elsewhere, particularly at Dublin, Cheltenham and Bath. Maud Watson, a parson's daughter, was the first Wimbledon champion. Her father was the vicar of Berkswell, Warwickshire and Maud defeated her elder sister Lilian in that first final. Another early Wimbledon star, Blanche Bingley, was born in Stratford, Middlesex and lived in upmarket Portland Place in central London. Charlotte Cooper and Lottie Dod were two other significant tennis players of the Victorian and Edwardian period (see the Case Studies chapter).

It will be noted that all these ladies came from comfortable backgrounds and there is little doubt that lawn tennis was a sport for those who did not need to spend time in manual labour. At the same time, it was not the mass-media sport it is today. As mentioned in the introduction to this book, when Charlotte Cooper returned successfully from one of her Wimbledon singles victories, a brother enquired as to whether she had been up to anything interesting that day!

Wimbledon also had rivals in the early days of lawn tennis. The confusingly named 'All England Women's Singles and Mixed Doubles' Championships' were played at Buxton in Derbyshire from the 1880s to the 1950s. These championships were 'much sought after', as were the Northern Championships held alternately at Liverpool and Manchester. Dublin, where the first ladies singles tournament was held in 1879, was said to host a festival as prestigious as Wimbledon itself.

For the majority of tennis players the game was played at club and county level and also enjoyed considerable popularity during the inter-war years. One of the great tennis clubs was Ealing Lawn Tennis Club. Their website claims, not without reason, that its 'history is almost the history of lawn tennis in this country'. It was founded in Ealing in 1882 as both a tennis and archery club, though there was eventually a falling out and the archers moved. The tennis club gained new premises in the Edwardian period and produced a number of successful Wimbledon tennis stars. Its own championships date from 1884. Buxton in Derbyshire, mentioned above, claims a tennis link to the cricket club that predates lawn tennis itself, and the town was overwhelmed by the interest shown in the competitions held in its gardens in the early 1880s.

For researchers into female tennis ancestry there remains one confusion. Tennis was a sport played by married and single women alike, and many ladies entered competitions after marriage under their new names. Histories of clubs and competitions do not always acknowledge this and it is possible to find the same person treated as two separate individuals.

Charlotte Cooper, for example, was one of the female sportswomen who played her career under two names. In 1901 she became Mrs Sterry and subsequently played the rest of her competitive career under that name. She also followed a route taken by many ladies in the Victorian and Edwardian periods by joining a local tennis club. (Indeed, the author found the names of two of his maternal grandmother's female first cousins in a handwritten membership book from our local lawn tennis club, dated 1886.)

Charlotte Cooper was a lively character known to all as 'Chattie'. Tall and lithe, her sporting life was devoted to tennis. Born in Ealing, Middlesex to an American mother, she took up the relatively new sport of lawn tennis at her local club. In 1895 she won the ladies single title at Wimbledon, just over a decade after the first women's final was played. By 1908 she had won the title five times and continued to play in the competition until 1912 when she was 41. She played competitive tennis until she was in her 50s (see the Olympics section at the end of this chapter).

WATER POLO

Water polo took root towards the end of the mid-Victorian period as a form of entertainment at swimming galas. By the 1890s the sport had gained passionate support in certain areas, nowhere more so than in Manchester where the team from Osborne Street Baths won the national title every year from 1894 to 1900.

International water polo actually came into being during the final decade of the twentieth century with teams from England, Ireland, Scotland and Wales all active by 1900. A club championship developed from 1888, the Otter and Burton Clubs being early victors. A county championship followed eight years later with Lancashire proving outstandingly strong. Lancastrians also enjoyed success as water polo-playing Olympians.

Many swimmers made the transition from competitive swimming to water polo. Early Olympian Henry Taylor is a classic case. John Henry Derbyshire (1878–1938), who was known as Rob, excelled in water polo – which he played and coached – as well as winning Olympic freestyle medals, holding a number of world records and coaching swimming. Like

Taylor he was from Manchester, the son of a baths attendant and connected to Osborne Street Baths.

WEIGHTLIFTING

Weightlifting developed as a competitive sport in the 1890s and was boosted by its inclusion in the first of the modern Olympics in 1896. The first world championships were held in London in 1891 and the early British stars were Launceston Elliot and Lawrence Levy (1851–1892). Elliot was the first Briton to win an Olympic event. Levy (christened Edward Lawrence) came from the Jewish community and won the first world championship against stiff international opposition. He was also the first British amateur weight-lifting champion and holder of numerous world records. He founded the Amateur Gymnastic Federation of Great Britain and Ireland. He was later inducted into the International Jewish Sports Hall of Fame.

As with many sports, weightlifting had early teething problems and some of the competition rules were unclear and the judging arbitrary. There was heated discussion over the nature of the equipment and the number of hands required to make the lifts.

WINTER SPORTS

Winter sports in Britain, especially those involving outdoor activity, have taken a relatively small foothold – mainly because of the nature of the British climate. Furthermore, mass involvement in such sports, and those of an Alpine nature in particular, is more a feature of the middle to late twentieth century. The fillip of a specific Winter Olympics also came relatively late, with one or two of the indoor 'winter sports' first appearing as part of the Summer Olympics.

All this noted, the Ski Club of Great Britain was set up as early as 1903. Vivian Caulfield (1874–1958) and Arnold Lunn (1888–1974) were both influential in the sport about this time, and the first important British ski race was held in 1911 – in Montana. Caulfield wrote a key textbook that updated attitudes towards the use of ski sticks. Lunn was Indian-born and died in London. He was the son of a Methodist minister who later became a renowned holiday organiser. Lunn is credited with the invention of slalom racing in the 1920s.

Initial Olympic and international participation interest lay in Nordic and cross-country winter sports. The move to Alpine and downhill sport gained a wider audience and led eventually to wider participation. Britain won a silver medal in the bobsleigh event at the first Winter Olympics in 1924. The side was made up of Thomas Arnold, Ralph Broome, Alexander Richardson and Rodney Soher. Buckinghamshire-born Richardson (1887–1964) was the son of an inventor and was an army officer with a distinguished war record.

WRESTLING

Despite the popularity of the professional sport in the nineteenth century, the amateur sport was very much a twentieth-century one. The National Amateur Wrestling Association was formed in 1904, becoming the British Amateur Wrestling Association towards the end of the Second World War.

Wrestling is a good example of the conflict that could take place between amateur and professional. When amateur interest began to grow towards the end of the nineteenth century, those who had competed for money prizes or wagers were banned. According to one source, the money was not at the heart of the matter; the 'professionals', most of them working men, were simply too good for the amateurs of the leisured classes and this was resented. It affected the standard of wrestling at the first Olympic Games held in Athens in 1896. However, one Scotsman did compete in the first wrestling event of the modern Olympic Games. This was Launceston Elliot, the successful weightlifter who was knocked out of the competition in the first round.

As with boxing, the number of different weights was limited during the early years. Among the first champions was Bert Sansom at bantamweight in 1909 and 1910, with other members of the Sansom family enjoying success after the First World War. Percy Cockings dominated the welterweight division before the war. Important clubs included the Hammersmith Amateur Wrestling Club.

OLYMPICS

A surprising number of British folk took part in the early modern Olympics. In fact the growth of the modern Olympics from 1896 onwards has a great deal to do with what was happening in amateur sport in Britain in the late Victorian period. Thus the early modern Olympics involved large numbers of people participating in British amateur sport, especially at the London Olympics of 1908. As for de Coubertin, the founder of the modern Olympics, the Corinthian spirit he observed in British school sport fired him up as did a visit to the rather quirky Much Wenlock Games (see below).

There is also a possibility of even earlier Olympian ancestors in the family – especially if that ancestry is to be found in either the Cotswold or Shropshire areas. Sadly, however, little is known about named individuals who participated in these games. These so-called Cotswold 'Olimpicks' were the brainchild of a Norfolk lawyer called Robert Dover (1575–1641) who arranged a sports meeting on a Cotswold hillside in 1612. Over the ensuing years the sports included sword fighting, wrestling and various throwing events. In addition there were, at times, horse racing, hunting and coursing. For these events, people were said to have travelled within a 60 mile radius of Dover's Hill, which overlooked the village of Weston Subedge.

These Olimpicks were still going in the nineteenth century, though by then they had gained a reputation for roughness. Wrestling had evolved into a form of shin kicking with competitors often wearing boots with sharpened nails. After one sword fight in the 1840s between Ebenezer Prestage of Campden and Mr Syres of Mickleton the unfortunate Syres died as a result of injuries sustained during the contest. Prestage was a well-known sportsman of his day (and his surname a common one in the Cotswolds). By the late nineteenth century enclosure had enveloped the land where the games had taken place and they died out until revival in a slightly different form in recent years.

About the time of the decline, William Penny Brookes began the 'Wenlock Olympian Class' at Much Wenlock in Shropshire. Sports played here included football, cricket, quoits, hopping, high jump and foot racing. De Coubertin attended the 1890 'class' and began his own Olympics six years later.

As indicated above, quite a substantial number of British sportsmen and women took part in the Olympics in the early days (between 1896 and 1924). The aim here is not to provide a complete biographical list but to explore areas of sporting ancestry that might well be worth following up.

The early Games (and those prior to the First World War in particular) took place in a world that was very different from today. Without radio, television or passenger flight, limited communication ensured that some heroes of the early modern Olympics remained fairly anonymous. This applies particularly to team sports where teams were often entered from entire clubs, with football and rugby providing good examples.

At the Paris Games of 1900 the British football representatives were Upton Park FC. Despite the professional side West Ham being associated with a ground of that name, this was not an early West Ham AFC side. Drawn from amateur players from the East End of London, the team defeated a French side to take first place.

Rugby Union, which had started after the split of rugby into League and Union, was another feature of the early modern Olympics. In 1900 the British representatives were Moseley Wanderers, whose players all came from the Midlands of England. The team came second to France in front of a crowd of 6,000. Playing that day was Arthur John Lovett Darby (1876–1960), who was the son of the archdeacon of Chester and later represented England in a home international game. Nicholas Jacob Tregurtha (1884–1964) was born in Penzance and Thomas Grenfell Wedge (1881–1964) is buried in Lelant – both in Cornwall. They were in the 'silver' medal-winning side at London in 1908, a time when Cornish rugby was very strong.

Cricket was only played once in the Olympics and, as chance had it, only in the form of a single game (see the Case Studies chapter). This was at the Paris Olympics of 1900 and the twelve young men in the team were all in a touring side called the Devon and Somerset Wanderers. They were all from the twin counties and amateurs drawn from a number of clubs. Only two of the side played cricket at first-class level at any point in their careers.

Yachting was an important early Olympic event and required large crews in certain classes. The list of competitors is thus quite long, especially for the 1908 Olympics based in London – with the races held off the Isle of Wight. Four classes were contested: 6m, 7m, 8m and 12m, with Great Britain taking gold in all four and other medals too.

Many of the successful crews are easy to follow up as they came from the same club. The 12m crew of the *Hera*, for example, was Scottish and included John Buchanan (1884–1943), a farmer from Rhu, and Arthur Downes, who had just recently qualified as a doctor. All were members of the Royal Clyde Yacht Club, one of the most important of the early sailing clubs. There were only two entrants for this particular competition. The other crew came from Merseyside and a coin toss took pace to decide where the competition should be held. The Clyde crew won so this contest took place north of the border.

With the Isle of Wight dominant in terms of yachting it is hardly surprising to find many competitors based there or nearby. Other yacht club members involved came from the Royal Victoria Yacht Club, the Royal Yacht Squadron and the Royal Burnham Yacht Club.

Rowing is another sport where success came to teams or crews. At the 1908 Olympics fours and eights both enjoyed success, as did the eights at Stockholm in 1912. The fours continued to succeed at Olympic level after the First World War. In the 1908 eights, the Leander club represented Britain and included Albert Gladstone (1886–1967), grandson of the famous prime minister and later a successful businessman. Guy Nickalls (1866–1935) was Surrey-born, one of a family of twelve and a rowing family at that. Raymond Etherington Smith (1877–1913) was a doctor from Putney. The fours were all from Magdalen College, Oxford and included John Somers Smith (1887–1916), a Surrey man who was to serve bravely in the First World War and died on the first day of the Somme.

Olympic rowing was one of the sports that crossed the class divide and entered the otherwise professional tradition of the single sculler. This was particularly the case with Harry Blackstaffe (1868–1951). An Islington-born butcher, Blackstaffe was one of the finest oarsmen of his day and capable of beating the best produced by the university and public school system. An amateur, he won gold at the 1908 London Olympics and was later made a Freeman of the City of London.

There was a similar mix in athletics. John Thomas Rimmer (1878–1962) won medals at the Paris Olympics in 1900 in the individual steeplechase and in the team event. Born in Lancashire, he was a Liverpool policeman and living in a lodging house at the time of the 1901 census. He ran for Sefton Harriers and late Stockport Harriers. George Larner (1875–1949) was a Buckinghamshire-born policeman who worked in Brighton. One of the most successful race walkers of all time, he won two golds at the 1908 London Olympics while two other British athletes – Ernest Webb and Edward Spencer – also gained medals. Grantley Goulding (1874–1944), on the other hand, was the son of a Gloucestershire farmer of 600 acres when he competed in the hurdles at Athens in 1896 (see also the Case Studies chapter for examples of Lincolnshire athletes).

As noted elsewhere in this chapter, Britain had many entrants and consequent success in boxing at the 1908 London Olympics. The victor in the middleweight class was J.W.H.T. Douglas (1882–1930), nicknamed 'Johnny Won't Hit Today' – not due to his involvement in boxing but because of his further sporting prowess as an Essex and England cricketer (he captained his country at one point). He also represented England as an amateur footballer and in many ways stood for the amateur Corinthian spirit of sport as it was perceived at the time. He died a hero, trying to save the life of his father after a shipwreck (his father was an important ABA official and had officiated at the 1908 competition). At the same Games, the lightweight class was won by Fred Grace (1884–1964), who later became ABA champion on a number of occasions. He was born in Middlesex, died in Essex and worked as a heating engineer. Richard Gunn (1871–1961) was champion in the featherweight division. He lived and died in London, working in the family tailoring business. He was almost 38 when he gained his Olympic crown and also succeeded at the ABA championships. Harry Thomas (1888–1963) was 1908 champion at bantamweight. He was Birmingham-born and later moved to the United States. Heavyweight champion Albert Oldman (1883–1961) served in both the police and the army.

Medals were awarded at the time but the regime of gold, silver and bronze as we know it did not come into being (including retrospective medals) until just before the First World War. Boxing returned to the Olympics after the war with Harry Mallin (1892–1969) taking gold in Antwerp in 1920 and in Paris in 1924. Ronald Rawson (1892–1952) took the gold at heavyweight in Antwerp. A public school Corinthian, he was only in the sport for a brief time and had excelled in other sports in his youth. Harry Mitchell (1898–1983) headed the light heavyweight division in Paris.

Wrestling is another Olympic sport of interest. At the 1908 London Olympics there were five different classes in the freestyle wrestling and Britain took eleven of the fifteen medals available. William Press (5ft 3in and 117lbs) took second place in the bantamweight division. He had four fights in all, the first three against British opponents Harold Witherall, Bruce Sansom and Frederick Tomkins.

Two other sports with a large number of British participants were water polo and tug of war. Britain was strong at water polo, taking first place in 1900, 1908, 1912 and 1920. In 1900 all the players were members of Manchester's highly successful Osborne Swimming Club. George Wilkinson (1879–1946), also a Manchester man, was in three of the winning teams. Welshman

Paul Radmilovic (1886–1968) was a swimmer and water polo player who held the British record for Olympic participation until the appearance of Sir Steve Redgrave in the late twentieth century. He had a Greek father and an Irish mother, and captained the Olympic water polo side on four occasions.

Tug of war featured as an Olympic event from 1900 to 1920, with many British participants and five medals (two gold, two silver and two bronze). Since entries were accepted from clubs rather than countries in this event, it was possible for a country to win three medals in one year of the Games. Great Britain did exactly that in 1908 when the City of London Police took first place, the City of Liverpool Police second and the Metropolitan Police K Division third – making for twenty-seven unlikely Olympic medallists. The names of all twenty-seven are known. The Liverpool team included Irish-born Patrick Philbin (1874–1929) and the London side Frederick Goodfellow (1874–1960). Cambridgeshire-born Goodfellow was living in Newington as a policeman age 26 in 1901.

Fencers won a silver medal for the Épée at the 1908 Games. The team of four included Charles Leaf Daniell (1877–1913), who was born in London and died on the Scottish borders.

Women first competed in the Olympic Games in 1900, in the tennis programme, although there were women involved with some of the larger boats in the sailing events (in 1908 the Duchess of Westminster took a keen interest in the yachting events without actually participating). In 1904, at St Louis, women had their own archery competition and were again present in 1908. At the St Louis Games of 1904 there were female boxers. Three female swimming and diving events were introduced in 1912.

Archery is possibly of most interest here. There were twenty-five British entrants for the ladies' archery contest in London in 1908. These formed the complete group of entries so, inescapably, Britain won gold, silver and bronze. Rochdale-born 'Queenie' Newall won the archery gold. She was almost 54 years old and remains the oldest female gold medal winner. The silver was won by former tennis player Lottie Dod (see the Case Studies chapter). The bronze was taken by Beatrice Hill-Lowe (1868–1951), a member of the Archers of Teme club based in the Welsh borders. She was born in Ireland and died in Wales. The club was founded in the 1850s and, though small, has an interesting history. There were two classes for men and one for women at these Games. Medals were awarded to ladies for what was known as the National Round where contestants fired several arrows at targets set at both 50yds and 60yds. In the days before passenger flight, few could afford the time to travel (or the money for it), and there were relatively few American contestants present.

The names of all twenty-five archery contestants can be viewed in many places online. Jessie and Brenda Wadworth competed as mother and daughter. Born in Wiltshire, they were living in the Welsh borders at the time of the 1901 census. Gertrude Appleyard was another contestant, thought to have been born in 1865. The only one of that name and appropriate age in the 1901 census appears to be the unmarried daughter of a Liverpool professor of music. Only one Albertine Thackwell (born in the 1860s and daughter of the chaplain to the workhouse, living in Alcester in the Midlands) turns up in relevant census returns. She finished fifteenth in the contest. Sixteenth was a familiar name – Doris Day – not the actress but probably the Welsh-born wife of a vicar in the Church of England.

Tennis was another sport that had female participants in the early years. Chattie Cooper (see the Case Studies chapter), victorious at Paris in 1900, has a special place in Olympic history as the first woman to win an Olympic event. At the same Games she also took the tennis mixed double title, partnering Englishman 'Reggie' Doherty.

Gladys Eastlake Smith (1883–1941) was another tennis medal winner. Born, like so many successful tennis players, in Surrey, she died in rural Yorkshire. As with other female players she continued to play after marriage – as Gladys Lamplough. Her success came in London in 1908 in the indoor singles, where she defeated fellow Briton Angela Greene in the final.

As noted in the section on amateur tennis, most of the competitive tennis players came from the leisured classes. This applied to the much-vaunted Doherty twins, Reggie and Hugh. The sons of a parliamentary printer, they enjoyed both Olympic and Wimbledon success and were held up in the textbooks of the day as a fine examples for budding tennis players to follow.

Women also enjoyed success in the ice-skating competitions held at the 1908 London Olympics. Madge Syres (see the Case Studies chapter) took gold in the individual and a bronze in the pairs. Dorothy Greenhough-Smith was third in the singles and Phyllis Johnson (1886–1967) second in the pairs.

Olympic swimming forms a neat contrast to many of the other early modern Olympic sports, as numerous participants came from the working class. Britain had swimmers in two Olympics pre-First World War: in Paris in 1900 and Stockholm in 1912. A classic example of this is Leicester girl

Jennie Fletcher (1890–1968), who won a bronze in the freestyle and a gold in the relay. She was said to be working some seventy hours a week in a factory at the time. Fittingly, she now features on Leicester's Walk of Fame.

There were three swimming events for females in 1912: a freestyle 100m, a freestyle relay and a static board diving contest. Leicester man Jack Jarvis (1872–1933) specialised over distance and won medals swimming in the Seine at the Paris Olympics in 1900. He won six Olympic medals in all and was part of the successful British water polo team at Paris that year. Manchester's Henry Taylor (1885–1961), who swam at Chadderton Swimming Club and later at the Hyde Seal Club, won numerous Olympic swimming medals. Like Jennie Fletcher, he came from a working-class background and did much of his training in canals and rivers close to his workplace, only using swimming baths on occasions when entrance fees were reduced. His Olympic successes eventually led to a posthumous entry into the Swimming Hall of Fame in the USA.

As a footnote, the first Olympic event won by a Briton was weightlifting at the Athens Games of 1896. Launceston Elliot (1874–1930) was the successful lifter and had already taken the world championship when it was held in London earlier in the decade. His success came in the two-handed lift – a success he was unable to repeat in either wrestling or rope climbing at the same Games. He also entered the discus at the ensuing Paris Olympics.

HOW TO RESEARCH
SPORTING ANCESTORS

The aim of this section of the book is to examine as many different types of useful resource as possible. Such is the extent of sporting history that a detailed analysis of all the available evidence is out of the question, so examples have been chosen from specific sports. This has been done under the general understanding that similar material may be available for other sports. Detailed references to 'chapter and verse' have been kept to a minimum in most cases as all the relevant details can be found in the final section of the book.

The study of history in general deals with two major types of source material – primary and secondary. Primary evidence was produced during the period of history being studied or at a later date by somebody who was there at the time. Secondary evidence is produced at a later (often *much* later) date, usually by someone who was not there at the time and has thus used primary evidence to build up a picture. A Victorian tennis player's diary and an Edwardian sporting newspaper would be good examples of primary evidence. Late twentieth-century books entitled *The Victorians and Tennis* and *The Sporting Press in Edwardian Times* would both be secondary. The division into primary and secondary is used in this chapter. Both are useful to the family historian but also have their own problems in terms of reliability. Where necessary, the evidence has been divided into written and pictorial categories, both of which are self-explanatory.

Primary Written and Oral Evidence

Many useful books were written by contemporary sportsmen and women either as autobiographies or as guidebooks to their particular sport. The Victorian runner, Walter George, for example, wrote on athletics and distance training after retiring, and a number of sporting personalities contributed to *The Badminton Library* series that began to come out towards the end of the Victorian period. This was an enormous enterprise, which culminated in over thirty volumes dedicated to individual sports (although a weakness with this series is that it deals mainly with the sports played by the upper classes).

Gloucestershire-based archer Horace Ford wrote about the history and skill of archery in the 1850s and there is also an excellent book on contemporary curling produced in Scotland during the Victorian period. Interesting cricket books from the time include reflective ones by Lancashire's R.G. Barlow in 1908, Surrey's William Caffyn in 1899 and overseas tour organiser Fred Lillywhite in the middle of the nineteenth century.

Informative articles can also turn up in the strangest of places, such as copies of the *Police Budget* for 1902–04, which contain a remarkably detailed series on boxing entitled 'Famous Fights – Past and Present'. This series of articles has already proved useful to family historians.

Many schools in which competitive sport was played in Victorian and Edwardian times produced their own magazines. These would cover not only interschool matches but also internal inter-house matches involving players of lower sporting ability. Twentieth-century copies of *The Salopian* magazine of Whitchurch Grammar School proved very useful for one researcher (see the Case Studies chapter), while an account of a rugby match from *The Blundellian*, produced by Blundell's School in Devon around 1900, gives some idea of what to expect from such publications:

'Football' – Blundell's *v.* All Hallow's School
at Honiton 'Won by 56 points to nil'

We started uphill and attacked at once; at his third attempt, Mainprice got in and kicked a goal. Soon afterwards Kingdon, from a pass from Mainprice, scored a try. Some excellent passing was then spoilt by Kingdon, and we rushed back, but for only a moment. Good passing brought the ball to Sahler, who ran well and nearly scored. From a scrum close on their line Gulston easily dodged in a try. Then Mainprice ran and added another goal. A clever run of Mainprice, and a neat pass to Ward, who was following well, enabled the latter to score a try. Half time 19 points to nil.

The names and initials of the players and their positions were given at the end of the report; H. Mainprice, S.P. Kingdon, H.G. Sahler, A.S. Gulston and W.D. Ward are all mentioned in the extract (the tendency of the wealthier to give their sons at least two names is helpful to the family historian when initials are the only additional details given). The 1901 census reveals three Mainprice brothers at Blundell's. They were Humphrey (18), Rupert (16) and Geoffrey (15). All three were born in Cheshire and Googling them reveals that Humphrey went on to play first-class cricket for Gloucestershire.

Elsewhere in the same edition of *The Blundellian* a former pupil gives an account of an adult cricket tour, which involved other ex-pupils. In other editions of the same magazine there are pen pictures of sporting pupils. These can often be amusing as they provided sports masters with the opportunity of getting their own back at 'characters' and poor trainers. Today, schools such as these may have archivists who will answer enquiries; otherwise somebody in the history department may take an interest – especially if ancestral achievements add to the school's reputation. Past copies of magazines may be held in a regional archive or at a local library or studies centre.

Contemporary newspapers – national, local and sport specific – are well worth consulting, depending of course on the standard of ancestral sport played. Sport has always sold newspapers although, in some cases, it is advisable to be prepared for disappointment. National newspapers have been going for centuries but tend to tackle the major sports and reference top sportsmen and women only. Copies of most of these can be viewed at the Colindale site of the British Library.

With the local and regional newspapers, which began to spring up in numbers during the Victorian period, it is a matter of pot luck. In the days before radio, television and telephone, the main aim of the local press was to keep readers informed on matters of importance. In a port town or city, for example, much space would be taken up with shipping affairs – movement of vessels, the weather and shipping disasters – also national and international news and, from the Crimean War onwards, war correspondence. Local Saturday games of cricket, rugby and football might not appear until Tuesday if other news demanded this – and sometimes would not appear at all if space did not allow.

Football.

BLUNDELL'S v. MR. R. G. VAUGHAN'S XV.
September 26, on the Tiverton Ground.
Lost by 30 points to 3.

A strong lot had been collected against us, and there was much anxiety to see how the new blood would acquit themselves. Blundell's started strongly, and by some fine forward rushes forced a couple of saves in the first five minutes, but then the turn of the scratch team came, and after a hot attack Sandford got possession, and proving too strong for our defence, scored (goal added). Equal play ruled for some time, Mainprice and Gwyther showing good form for us; then Gulston made a strong rush through all the forwards, and after a scramble near the line, scored far out. A splendid attempt at goal struck the post. On resuming the scratch team again pressed, and scored through Berry, the kick being successful. Half time arrived with the score 3 points to Blundell's, 10 to opponents.

So far the game had been very even, but soon after half time the weakness of our lines of defence became sadly evident. In spite of good efforts by Drake and Archer the forwards slackened their efforts in collaring, and the three-quarters seemed quite unable to cope with a determined rush. The Sandford brothers, Vaughan, and Hughes each scored after good runs, and two other tries were made out of scrums; so that, one of these tries being converted, Blundell's were defeated by 30 points to 3.

Team.—H. M. Veitch, back; S. P. Kingdon, A. H. Duckett, C. E. Gwyther, J. L. Thomas, threequarters; H. Mainprice, A. S. Gulston, halves; H. Archer, W. W. Nind, W. D. Ward, T. J. Read, A. J. Symes, P. J. Vincent, J. C. B. Drake, C. H. Smith, forwards.

BLUNDELL'S v. ALL HALLOW'S SCHOOL.
At Honiton, October 16.
Won by 56 points to nil.

We started uphill and attacked at once; at his third

A Victorian school rugby match, *The Blundellian*, 1900. (Author's collection)

A fine example of sporting coverage can be found in *The Illustrated London News* for Saturday 5 August 1882. One page alone (p. 142) references sailing, archery, swimming, rowing, athletics and cycling. Among the people mentioned here is a Miss Isabella Carter, an archer who achieved the largest number of gold hits at the Grand National Archery Meeting.

Even when match reports do appear in local newspapers, they might not be totally reliable or informative. This is particularly true of early football reports. In some of these reports, it can even be difficult to work out whether it is rugby football or association football being played. In most cases surnames alone were given and these were frequently misspelt. Equally, when Christian names appear in print they can be inaccurate. All this noted, local newspapers are definitely worth consulting, though the type of research required can often be arduous and unrewarding. Local newspapers are generally found in local study libraries and regional archives – frequently on microfilm, well indexed and easy to access.

As time progressed, so did coverage of major local sporting events and, in addition to this, weekly columns dedicated to sporting reviews. Previews began to appear. These are worth looking out for as the correspondent frequently refers to team selection and names individuals in the case of team sports. These columns usually appeared on the same day every week with Thursdays and Fridays especially favoured. In some cases the newspapers have been indexed and the name of a team or even a player may be found there. There is no doubt that local newspapers have their uses. For example, in his centenary history of Droitwich Golf Club (1893–1993), writer John Bromhead quotes the magnificently named *Droitwich Guardian and Brine Baths Recorder* as a key resource.

It is also worthwhile examining newspapers, and especially local ones, for obituaries. If the date of death of a sporting ancestor is known then this should not be an arduous task as obituaries appeared, invariably, soon afterwards. 'Well-known in the sporting community' was a popular phrase with obituary writers from Victorian times onwards, and the more popular the sportsman or woman the more likely the obituary was to have sold newspapers.

During the period covered by this book there were literally hundreds of sporting magazines and newspapers, and many of them were relatively short-lived. Mike Huggins provides a comprehensive list in his key work on Victorian sport. A sample trawl through his book leads to publications such as the *Bicycling News and Tricycling Gazette*, *Illustrated Sporting and Dramatic News*, *Cricket and Football Times*, *Bell's Sporting Life*, *Sporting Chronicle*, *Sporting Life*, *Sporting Magazine*, *Swimming* and *Rowing and Athletic Record*.

As far as starting dates for major magazines are concerned, the following give some idea: *Sporting Press* (1853), *The Field* (1859), *Sporting Life*
(1865), *Athletics News* (1875) and *Cricket* (1882). The main sporting interest
of the early Victorian press lay in horse racing, coursing, yachting, cricket
and rowing. The most popular sporting paper was *Bell's Life In London,
and Sporting Chronicle*, which predated Victoria and ran until the 1880s.
Appearing at various times as a weekly and daily publication, *Bell's Life* is
an obvious starting point for anyone researching a reasonably successful
Victorian sporting ancestor. *Sporting Life*, which ran from the middle of the
nineteenth century to the end of the twentieth century (and was eventually
absorbed *Bell's Life*) is another handy resource.

The great cricketing publication *Wisden's Almanack* also comes under this
heading. An annual publication from 1864, it covers everything concerning
first-class cricket and beyond, and includes articles by contemporaries. It
is also packed with details of the deeds of amateurs and professionals past
and present. Early matches covered in detail include The Gentlemen of the
MCC vs Royal Engineers (1871), North vs South (1872) and Huntsmen of
England vs Jockeys (1880). The last game, a draw, was played with thirteen
aside, eleven of whom are mentioned in the account. Past copies of *Wisden*
were condensed into anthologies in the late twentieth century with the
1864–1900 edition possibly the most useful to the family historian.

Magazines and newspapers produced for younger readers can also contain
information of use to the family historian. The *Boy's Own Paper*, published
weekly, had regular sports-related articles. It kept up to date with football,
cricket and rugby in the public schools and published photographs and pen
pictures of players. It also kept up with football and cricket in state schools
in Edwardian times and provided information on competitions in schools
in metropolitan London.

Match programmes, scorecards and scorebooks can also help flesh
out the bones of sporting ancestors, although the match programme is a
frustratingly modern concept belonging firmly to the twentieth century
rather than nineteenth century and earlier. The monetary value placed on
pre-Second World War football programmes is an indication of the rarity
of those that have survived. In the Ashbrooke archives, Sunderland, there
are programmes for county rugby finals and tennis competitions from the
1920s. There are also single sheet programmes for late nineteenth-century
Whitsuntide cycling and athletic sports, but they list events alone and
not the names of competitors. The collecting of football programmes is a

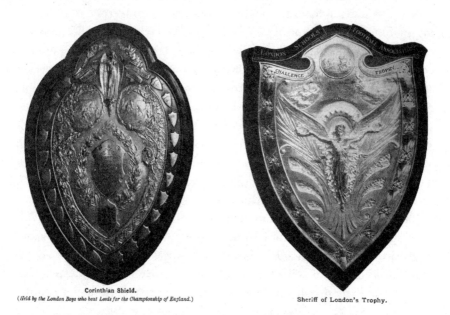

Corinthian Shield.
(Held by the London Boys who beat Leeds for the Championship of England.)

Sheriff of London's Trophy.

Trophies for late Victorian school football contests in *Boy's Own Paper*.

Elementary Schools Champions of England, 1901.

The winners of a late Victorian school football trophy in *Boy's Own Paper*.

serious hobby with a number of sites dedicated to it and many old football programmes can be found at the British Library site at Colindale.

Scorecards were provided at first-class cricket matches and some of these have survived and may be viewed in local club archives and repositories. A well-organised local cricket club may also have kept its original scorebooks – not only for the first XI but also for the second and third XIs, and even for the junior sides. Scorebooks from friendly matches can also be of interest with some games organised against teams normally associated with other sports and, on occasions, between male and female sides. Scorebooks have survived from Edwardian times and in some cases even earlier.

If the name of an ancestor's club is known then it may be worth looking through more recent match programmes, as there are frequently articles on club history and features on past players. The interest in family history has also led descendants of sportsmen and women from Victorian and Edwardian times into contacting clubs and subsequently being interviewed about their ancestors for magazine features. Many of the larger football clubs now produce glossy magazines for their season ticket holders at regular intervals and these too feature historical articles. England Rugby Supporters Club members receive a similar magazine.

Songs and ballads are a surprisingly good source for past sporting personalities, local and national. Sportsmen have long been the subject of popular rhyme and a surprising number of sportsmen, great and small, turn up in nineteenth-century street ballads – especially those who were wrestlers, cricketers, pedestrians, runners, rowers and boxers. The original ballad sheets are usually to be found in public archives and study centres, although many were published in collections in Victorian times. A number of these were reprinted in the twentieth century.

One surviving wrestling song is *A New Song of the Great Wrestling Match between Thomas Longmire and Richard Wright for the Champion Belt and £100*. This match took place at Ulverston, North Lancashire in 1851. The same year saw a fight which gave rise to a ballad entitled *The Wrestling Match Between Atkinson and Jackson* (Robert Atkinson of Westmorland and William Jackson of Cumberland). Another has the grandiose title *A New Song on the Great Wrestling Match for 50 pound A-Side between Taylor of Brampton and Taylor of Distington*. Each song started with the words 'Come All Ye' and each song was set to the same well-known tune of *The Nutting Girl*.

A fine cricket song, thirteen verses long, has survived from 1826, concerning a match played near Sheffield. The title is very informative, *A*

And shining tin-flasks of new milk, which seem
Best to demand the name of good thick cream !
   The dinner done ; the happy train so gay,
In various groups disperse to various play ;
Some to the hounded-hare the sinews strain,
And fleet as greyhounds scour along the plain.
At last the hare through all her windings caught
Gets leave to breathe, and breath brings change of thought ;
For races some, but more for foot-ball cry,
Mark out their ground, and toss the globe on high ;
The well fought field deals many a galling stroke,
And many a chief's o'erthrown, and many a shin is broke.
   These active feats, while manly imps essay,
The gentler sex choose out a gentler play ;
They form a smiling circle on the green,
Where chuckstones, dolls, and totums, all are seen ;
A nest of linnets, a few happy elves,
Run home to see if yet they pick themselves,
Though but an hour ago their throats they cramm'd,
And chirp'd, and cheep'd, and well the mother shamm'd.
   Escap'd in happy hour from rod-taught lore,
Their books forgot, nor work remember'd more ;
All share the joy, but one imprison'd slave,
Who from offended worth no boon would save.
The dame he said was like a clocking hen,
Who ne'er would let them out when it did rain ;
And if again his hands she dar'd to switch,
He'd call her to her face a wrinkl'd witch.
This told a wheedler, much dislik'd by all,
Whom in abhorrence they tale-pyet call,

Foot-ball in the eighteenth-century schoolyard as described in a poem by Susanna Blamire, *Poetical Works* (Carlisle, 1842).

Cricket Song on the Match when the Nottingham Club Played the Sheffield and Leicester Clubs at Darnall, July 1826, in which Marsden Scored from his Own Bat 227 Runs at One Innings. The author, a local writer, mentions 'Rawlins and Marsden', 'Old Father Dennis', 'Davis, Barber and Vincent', 'Gamble, Barber and Clarke' and 'Kettleband'. Tom Marsden made it into the *Cricketers' Who's Who*, while Clarke is probably the legendary touring professional William Clarke playing in one of his first games (see The Professionals chapter).

Pedestrians and runners formed a popular subject for songs; pedestrians appeared in early nineteenth-century street ballads and the Victorian professional runners in published songbooks. Geordie Ridley, author of *The Blaydon Races*, wrote a number of songs about local runners in the 1860s. He took a special interest in the sport as his brother, Stephenson (Stephen) Ridley, was the current 1 mile champion of England.

Professional boat rowers also appeared in song, including the Tyneside champions Harry Clasper, Bob Chambers and Jimmy Renforth. The Thames rowers turn up in these songs, too – often by the boatload. A broadsheet writer noted in 1842:

Coombes, Newell and Parish, the Pride of the Thames
Have in many boat races exalted their names

While Renforth went to race in Canada with a mixed Thames and Tyne crew and a named official:

Along with Kelley, Chambers, Bright, he crossed the deep blue sea
Along with Billy Oldham, the well known referee

A boat race on the Wear in 1863 led to references to a series of relative unknown rowers:

'Cud' Robson aye and Hutton tee
They sure will really have a spree
Leithead and Grievson looked sae weel
As from the Baron's Quay they did steal

Some of these songs have been recorded. A 1962 record on the Topic label features folk song collectors and singers A. L. Lloyd and Ewan McColl singing about Skewball (an eighteenth-century racehorse owned by Arthur

Marvell and raced in Kildare in Ireland). There are also two boxing songs; one on the fight between Tom Sayers and John Heenan at Farnborough in 1860 and the other concerning Irishman John Morrisey, born 1831, who was a well-known fighter in the USA in the 1860s.

In Scotland, the poet and balladeer Robert Burns was a keen curler and a ballad has also survived singing the praises of nineteenth-century Welsh athlete John Davies. Ballads and songs may seem rather a strange source for the family historian but it is remarkable what does turn up, as these examples show – and it is quite something to be remembered for sporting prowess in song.

Scrapbooks containing details of a sporting career can be extremely helpful, although it is difficult to predict exactly where they might turn up. Often they are in the possession of a descendant of the sportsman or woman concerned and were not necessarily put together by the person who participated in the sport. Supporters also kept team and individual records by cutting and pasting from the local press. This saves a considerable amount of trawling through newspapers. Such a scrapbook exists for every game played by Sunderland Rugby Union Club's first XV in the mid-1920s. A descendant of the enthusiast donated this to the club and the cuttings include not only match reports but also the weekly press reviews mentioned above.

A diary from the Second World War. (Author's collection)

Personal sporting archives and diaries are fairly rare yet, where they do exist, highly useful and informative. These personal archives may contain both written and pictorial material in the shape of photographs, press cuttings and medals. They can be a random collection kept in an old tin box or a carefully maintained file, either remaining with the family or handed over to an archive. One such family collection consists of rugby-related material belonging to a man who played rugby and cricket in the 1920s and refereed rugby at international level in later life. It was put together by a rugby-playing friend after his death and includes programmes, photographs, correspondence and press cuttings. One of the last of the great cricketing footballers, Chris Balderstone, kept and catalogued every piece of sporting memorabilia from childhood onwards.

Sporting diaries from Victorian times are to be truly treasured. There are diaries known to be kept by British competitors at the 1900 Paris Olympics and by cricketers on tour in Australia. In the latter instance the Reverend Vernon Royle, who toured Australia in 1878–9, kept a personal diary with entries such as:

First day of our match against 18 South Australians. In fact our first match in the Colonies. They went in first and made 110. Jarvis played best for them with 28. We got 106 for 4 wickets. Webbe 35 – Hornby 42 not out.

Jarvis was later to become Australia's second choice wicket-keeper, Webbe and Hornby were well-known English cricketers, while the reverend played for Lancashire and appeared once for England.

Royle was an amateur cricketer. For many of the working-class sporting professionals in the past, one of the main aims was to make future provision for themselves and their families. Professional careers in some sports were short and, in the case of certain contact sports, brutal and telling on the health. At the same time, success could bring with it considerable wealth in the form of prize money and benefits. Victorian newspapers are awash with details of benefit dinners and gala concerts held for retiring sporting personalities. Once the money was collected, the ideal way to spend it was on purchasing a public house or shop. Champion sculler Harry Clasper became a publican, as did many former prizefighters and boxers. Members of the sporting Nottinghamshire Daft family set themselves up as sports outfitters in the nineteenth century, as did Yorkshire cricketing footballer Willie Watson in the twentieth. Another Nottinghamshire cricketer, Mordecai Sherwin, was running the Alexander Inn in Nottingham in 1891. By then he was 40 years old. Will Ritson, legendary Cumberland and Westmoreland wrestler, ran a pub on the western fringes of the Lake District. As a result, the names of many ex-professional sportsmen may be found in selected trade directories. These exist for major urban areas from the early nineteenth century and even before in some cases (particularly for London). By the late Victorian period the directories were well established and it is possible to trace people in them by name, profession and address (both home and trade). Many of these books can still be found on the open shelves of local studies libraries and regional archives.

Archives may also throw up other printed material of use to the sporting family historian. Named sporting personalities were often mentioned on posters from the early days and beyond. This was certainly the case for boat racing where railway companies from the 1840s onwards would advertise trips alongside the river to watch the race. They also did this for the pedestrians of the early nineteenth century.

Perhaps one of the most intriguing forms of primary evidence comes under the oral heading. This resource, as might be expected, has a relatively short life-span. Older researchers may recall talking in their youth to elderly people who experienced Victorian and Edwardian sport firsthand. Today, as the twenty-first century advances, the most that can be expected is a tale of school-based activity in the years after the First World War and some adult sport (including the local leagues and competitions which were popular during these years.) The remaining memories are likely to be from the Second World War onwards. In some cases, the evidence presented may not be all that reliable as memories tend to fade. This noted, older folk are often capable of recalling events of sixty or seventy years ago with extreme clarity, even if they remain uncertain as to what happened the day before.

Early memories of school team sports such as football, rugby, cricket and hockey still abound and can often be backed up by accessing school magazines for the period in question. The same may be said of less popular sports such as fives, rackets and lacrosse. Oral accounts of Wednesday and Sunday league football matches may be followed up in the local newspaper, while the glorious mishmash that was football between 1939 and 1945 now has a number of written histories of its own. As noted elsewhere, wartime sport often brought the keen amateur and the seasoned professional together and, in peacetime, this became a badge worn with pride by the amateur for years after.

Oral tales can usually be backed up with family memorabilia or followed up by accessing the relevant book. Equally, amateur cricketers at a fairly mundane level may have played with the 'greats' of the day when such players served as club professionals, especially in the north of England. This was the case from the 1920s onwards and examination of club histories can usually back up tales relating to such an experience. When the inter-war generation passes on, they can at least leave their memories in the shape of recordings and interviews. Some recordings relating to sport during Victorian and Edwardian periods have survived. These are comparatively rare and must be treated as an exceptional bonus.

PRIMARY PICTORIAL AND VISUAL EVIDENCE

Photography developed at just the right pace to be able to record many of the major early developments in British sport. Experimented with in various countries in the early nineteenth century, the art was honed (in relation to human photography in particular) during the Crimean War of the 1850s and the American Civil War of the 1860s. It was thus in place to capture images of sports such as cricket and rugby as they settled down in the 1870s and '80s.

Early photographic images of sport tend to be studio based and, in true Victorian style, posed. Action photographs had to await further progress in the science of photography. This said, there are a number of curling-related photographs from the late Victorian period, which could almost be described as action pictures (see examples in the *Played in Britain* series). Team photographs of rugby sides dating from the 1870s and cricketing sides from even earlier turn up in archives, books and magazines. Photographs have survived of the professional cricket teams that toured Britain playing against the odds during mid-century, as well as the local XXIIs formed to play against them. Many of the early international sides were captured, as were notable (and less well known) sporting individuals. Many of the early British Olympians were photographed, too.

Original photographs, or copies of originals, are frequently displayed on the walls of corridors and bars in modern sports clubs. They turn up in public and club archives and also appear in published collections. Publishers like Batsford and David & Charles produced books of local interest in the late twentieth century, many of them based on original photographs alone.

One of the Batsford books dealing with Lancashire in the 1920s and '30s has a photograph of a team of curlers in Preston in 1938, and a golf match at Southport and Ainsdale in 1933, in addition to horse racing, cricket, football and Rugby League images. The same book includes a photograph of a javelin competition organised for the unemployed at a pre-war camp, set up by a committee of the joint Lancashire and Cheshire councils.

In a similar book on the history of the city of Durham, a section on 'Schooldays and Sport' features seventeen sporting photographs depicting sportsmen and women. The earliest photograph is dated 1908 and the most recent 1952. Sports featured include rowing, swimming and diving, rugby, judo and football. Interesting photographs include one of Elvet Wanderers football team in 1908 ('most parishes in the city had their own football teams') and a very young rugby side from St Margaret's School taken in 1911. It is not unusual to find entire sections dedicated to sporting history in such books and publications. The highly recommended English Heritage *Played in Britain* series is as much about photography as it is about the written word.

Photographs of sporting activity can turn up in the strangest places. In a contemporary book on Victorian and Edwardian sailors' missions, for example, there are photographs of a sailors' football team based at the Liverpool Mission, English sailors playing cricket at San Francisco and 'The Antwerp Chaplain with his sailors' football team'. The weekly *Boy's Own Paper* published photographs of successful workhouse and state school football and cricket sides in the Edwardian period and, in some cases, named the players. Greater Manchester County Record Office has a fascinating collection of photographs relating to roller skating and roller hockey between the wars. This includes one photograph of the British international roller skating team of 1924 with all the players named. The coach was A.R. Eglington who, according to the accompanying notes, 'won all the roller skate racing championships in 1923, 1924 and 1925'.

By the twentieth century sporting photographs were relatively common and the increased use of the postcard during the Edwardian period led to the 'snapping' of sporting sides of differing ability. It is not unusual to come across photographs of Wednesday and Sunday league teams from the inter-war years, and these constitute the kind of material likely to turn up in boxes of family memorabilia.

Moving images of early sport are rare and much valued. One of the earliest footballing images of this type involves a match between Blackburn Rovers and West Bromwich Albion in 1898, while the museum at Twickenham has film of early rugby internationals (the latter reveals how little work the old-fashioned forwards were prepared to do). There is film of various Derbies and boat races from the late Victorian period and, by Edwardian times, most sports were being featured where audiences were watching films. Individual sport museums and various film archives are worth a visit if it is thought that a sporting ancestor might have been filmed.

Prints and cartoons also became popular means of recording sportsmen and women, even after the introduction of photography. It is thus possible to find both prints and original drawings of early prizefighters and jockeys. James Gillray's portrayal of prizefighter 'Gentleman' John Jackson falls into this category, although it is worth noting that the racing prints tended to be more about the horse and owner than the jockey. Many of the famous prints published in *Vanity Fair* magazine were produced by the artist 'Spy'. These include billiards player John Roberts Jnr (in 1885), boxer Captain Edgeworth Johnstone (1896), cricketer Digby Jephson (1902), jockey George Barrett (1887) and rower William Fletcher (1893). Barrett (1863–98) is said to have been an astute man and made good use of his financial success. Digby Jephson (1871–1926) captained Surrey between 1900 and 1902. At that time he was playing as an amateur, working in the stock exchange and living in Clapham with his German-born wife and a servant. Captain W. Edgeworth Johnstone of the Royal Irish Regiment had been successful in the ABA championships during the year previous to his picture appearing in the magazine. Suffolk-born Barrett was in Newmarket as a jockey groom, aged 18, at the time of the 1881 census.

Cartoons of groups of sportsmen and sportswomen became popular in both local and national press in the years following the First World War. A local newspaper, for example, might feature tennis players in a competition, both male and female, or a rink of bowlers that had enjoyed success in a national competition. Such cartoons were often humorously cruel in picking out any prominent physical features and the drawings were frequently accompanied by jolly quips.

With the developing popularity of the cigarette came the very collectible cigarette card. Sets relating to individual sportsmen and women are still popular and collectible. Today, it is also possible to buy modern framed copies of such sets comprising some twenty to thirty sporting individuals each. They were also gathered together by the collectors themselves in small albums provided by the cigarette companies. Such collections include 'An Album of Cricketers, 1938' and 'Association Footballers, 1936–38'. Similar cards were also placed in sweet packets. The cigarette card was popular from the late nineteenth century up to the Second World War, when they were banned and never really recovered their popularity.

Some of the cigarette card collections deal with contemporary sportsmen and women. Others contain cards of sporting personalities from years past. A good example of this is John Player and Sons' 1939 collection relating to cycling over the previous century. There are fifty cards in all with a number of them featuring named cyclists. One shows Herbert Cortis on a penny-farthing in 1882 and another has Frederick Bidlake on his tricycle in the 1990s. There is also a card depicting the famous Smiths (J.S. and his wife); he not only made the machines, he also raced them and the pair held a number of distance records.

Card collections can still be picked up at car boot sale and antique fairs at a reasonable price and a modern American website quotes a standard price of $20–50 for a full set in a book. Prints, however, tend to be more expensive and can cost £100 or more. Images on cards and prints can often be picked up on the internet simply by Googling an image. There are also a large number of websites dedicated to card collection.

Also included in this section is visual evidence, which includes ephemera such as medals, cups and trophies. Medals won by top professionals and amateurs are much prized and can bring high prices in the salesrooms. Some remain with families while other may be exhibited in museums or even in glass cases in clubhouses. Local leagues had their rewards too in the shape of medals, and these can often be seen on photographs taken in the early twentieth century. Some of these were deliberately small and created to hang on a watch chain. Medals such as these are frequently marked with the date and the name of the league. Small, inscribed replica trophies were also handed out to team members in some cases (see the Case Studies chapter).

Original sporting equipment must be the icing on the cake of any family collection. This may include caps awarded for achievement, which may or may not be worn when playing (look out for them on photographs of rugby, football and cricket teams in particular). Caps such as these are often to be found on public display in museums and clubhouses. One family in northern England still possesses an ancestral county junior football cap and a club running vest, both dating from the late Victorian period. Ancient bats and racquets are a real rarity and should be cherished. In one popular television antiques programme, a lady appeared with a couple of boxes filled with nineteenth century golf balls and a photograph of an ancestor playing golf with the good and great of the sport in the Victorian era (including one of the Morris family). One of the golf balls was valued at £2,000, although, as the antique expert noted at the time, the golf ball was probably of much greater value to the family itself.

Secondary Written Sources

The internet's powerful search engines and ability to provide immediate information has undoubtedly fuelled a revolution in research. Some may argue that it has almost eliminated the need for books, yet there are still some who are not conversant or happy with modern technology and many more who find books reassuring, useful and handy. Books and booklets covering the history of sport can be picked up very cheaply in charity shops, second-hand bookshops and at car boot sales. They may also be found on the open shelves in the local library, stored in a basement archive or in collections in a separate local studies library. The following types of book should prove useful in seeking out sporting ancestors and understanding the nature of their sport.

General sports encyclopaedias have been produced regularly over the years, with publishers Sampson, Low and Marston publishing a particularly useful and informative one in the late 1950s. (Judging by the number of copies still around in second-hand shops, it was probably a popular Christmas present.) This work is packed with information on the history of sports major and minor, record holders and trophy winners. A large book of over 300 packed pages, it also has hundreds of illustrations and mentions thousands of sporting names – the vast majority from the British Isles. Individual sports also generally have their own encyclopaedias, with one on football produced by the *Daily Telegraph* in the late twentieth century highly recommended. To a great extent physical encyclopaedias have been overtaken by online encyclopaedias, which are constantly updated (see Modern Technology at the end of this chapter).

Before moving on to specific sports books, it is worth drawing attention to the ever growing number of titles in the thoroughly researched *Played in Britain* series. These are part of an ongoing project being carried out by English Heritage, which looks at sporting buildings in the context of the development of British sport. At the time of going to press, books have

Encyclopaedia of SPORT

4

A useful general sporting book – *Encyclopaedia of Sport* (1950s). (Author's collection)

been written on Manchester, Liverpool, Birmingham, Glasgow and Tyne and Wear, and the regional nature of the books should make them even more appealing to ancestral researchers. Although mainly about the architecture of sport, each volume goes into great detail about all the sports played in the area and the venues at which they were held. In each case all the major sports are dealt with, yet each separate volume manages to retain its own local flavour. The Manchester book, for example, has chapters on archery, real tennis and lacrosse. Lacrosse was (and still is) a sport which for some reason only gained popularity in certain areas, industrial Lancashire being one of them. The Birmingham book has a chapter dealing with skating – both ice and roller – and one on the links between local industry and the growth of cycling and motorcycling as sports in the English Midlands. The Tyne and Wear volume covers rowing and potshare bowling, as well as pigeon racing.

As with encyclopaedias, books on the history of individual sports are still relatively easy to lay one's hands on, such as Cleaver's *History of Rowing* and the Race Walking Association's history of its sport, produced in the 1950s and '60s respectively.

Cricket is a sport that goes hand in glove with the production of written material. Writers of different types have found it hugely attractive at all levels and the family historian is bound to gain from this. Cricket may also serve as a good example for the type of book that may turn up relating to other sports.

Most sports have their individual encyclopaedias, the most useful of which, from the family historian's point of view, are those based on short biographies of people who played the game. In the case of cricket this is the multi-authored *Cricketers' Who's Who*, first produced in the 1980s. Dealing with every known first-class cricketer who has played in England since the 1860s, it also references a significant number of cricketers who played before that. The following example shows the amount of detail which can be expected – even for the most humble of players:

Martin, Marcus Trevelyan – Amateur born 29.4.1842 Barrackpore, Calcutta, India – died 5.6.1908, Marylebone, London. He died of appendicitis. Middle-order right-hand batsman, wicket keeper. School Rugby. Teams Cambridge University (1862–64, blue 1862 and 1864), Middlesex (1870, 1 match) Career batting – 9 matches, 12 innings, 1 not out, 208 runs at an average of 18.90 – 8 catches and 6 stumpings. His first-class debut was for Gentlemen of

A useful book dedicated to a specific sport – *The Sport of Race Walking* (1950s).
(Author's collection)

the North in 1861. He also played non-first-class cricket for Warwickshire and Huntingdonshire.

There may also be a detailed history of the sport, which is usually packed with names. In the case of cricket, Altham and Swanton's *A History of Cricket* has been in print from the 1920s onwards and appears in the bibliography of most of the modern cricketing books. David Rayvern Allen is another well-respected cricket historian who produced informative works on Victorian and Edwardian cricket and cricket songs in the 1980s. Derek Birley's *Willow Wand* from the 1980s and David Kynaston's more recent celebration of W.G. Grace and friends are particularly useful in appreciating the difficulties faced in differentiating between amateur and professional cricketers in the past. Birley's work on all forms of sport is generally highly respected.

Some books will concentrate on players with a particular talent within a sport. In the case of cricket such a work is G.D. Martineau's *The Valiant Stumper*, a 1950s creation that has pen pictures of many wicket-keepers. There are also likely to be books dealing with the sport at a lower level. Gerald Howat writes about cricket on the village green from its birth to the latter years of the twentieth century. Some books may deal with the history of a specific fixture. Chesterton and Doggert's book on Oxford and Cambridge cricket covers the fixture right back to the 1820s.

While it could be argued that most books will deal with fairly well-known sporting personalities, smaller booklets often feature the less well known and are thus worth seeking out. Take for example those produced in recent years by the Association of Cricket Statisticians. Among these are booklets on Liverpool and District cricketers from 1882 to 1949, English cricketers who played first-class games overseas but not in England, and the touring team of Sir Julian Cahn, which started playing soon after the First World War. There is also a detailed booklet, published privately, on the only cricketers to play in the Olympic Games (in Paris in 1900).

Cricket is undoubtedly blessed with its literature but books on similar topics exist for many other sports and these are noted in the final section of this book. As might be expected, there has been a wealth of material published on footballing history in particular, and not least on players' records and where to find them. There are also numerous good chronicles and compendiums and an increasing number of detailed books covering individual subjects such as wartime football.

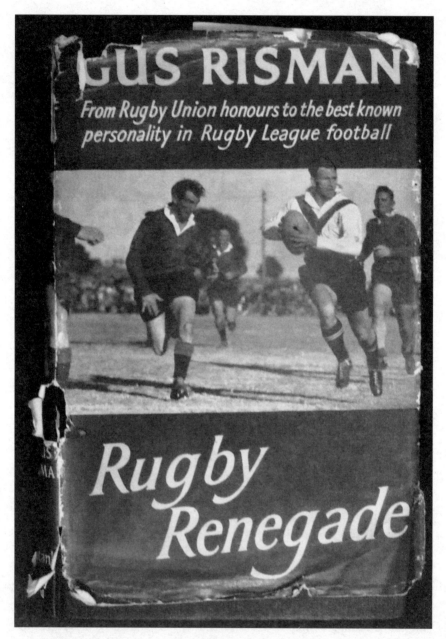

A useful biographical book – *Gus Risman* (1950s). (Author's collection)

Whereas autobiographies are primary sources, many biographies are secondary and often written long after the sporting personality has died. They are no less valuable to the family historian than contemporary works and a well-researched historical biography will direct readers to the primary sources used in its construction. References to the early years of famous sporting personalities can be particularly useful as they often bring in school sport and early careers at small local clubs. These are worth seeking out if a sporting ancestor had a particular connection with a school or club. The vast majority of successful sportsmen and women began their careers at a humble level, never forgot their roots, and were more than happy to visit them in the early chapters of their life stories.

Rugby legend Gus Risman played both League and Union during a long career and his book is packed with the names of those he met during it. Born in Cardiff in 1911, he first attended South Church Street School until, at the age of 11, he moved to Barry where his father opened a couple of cafes. Here he attended Gladstone Road School where in a class behind him was 'George Green who ... was later to play soccer for Charlton Athletic and Wales'. There was also a 'tiny chubby' young lad whose father was the local golf professional. Dai Rees was to leave his mark on the game of golf too. Gus then moved on to Barry Grammar School where he came across 'Ronnie Boon and Danny Evans', both of whom were to win rugby caps for Wales. After school he started his rugby career with a tiny club at Dinas Powys, before going to Cardiff Scottish (where 'expenses' were paid!). From there it was all up – into Lancashire, Rugby League and international honours. Gus's route and experiences in youth are far from unusual and similar works are worth exploring.

Some of these secondary biographies and histories can be quite early, as with the case of Robinson and Gilpin's account of wrestling published just before 1900, which actually deals with wrestlers from a much earlier age.

Many of the local histories published rely heavily on photographs as a sales point (see the previous section on photographs), but there remain many detailed works heavily dependent on the written word. A good example of this is Bill Myers' *Millom Revisited,* which deals with the story of the growth of a small Cumbrian town on the cusp of old Lancashire. The town came to life as a result of the discovery of workable iron in the nineteenth century and this brought workers flooding in to the mines – particularly from the redundant metal mines in Devon and Cornwall. The book has an entire chapter on sport and leisure, dedicated in the main to Rugby League, cricket and schoolboy football. The Rugby League section is particularly interesting as it deals with the oldest amateur club 'in the world': founded as a rugby club in 1873, Millom remained amateur during the league period. The chapter also includes a number of pen pictures of local rugby players. Among them is Bill Eagers, who played for Millom and village side Haverigg in the 1890s, before joining the professional ranks with Bradford and Hunslet. He gained one cap for England but was badly wounded in the First World War.

Many sports clubs have their own published histories and, in some cases, a number of them over the years. A good example of this is the 256-page history of association football side Carlisle United, *The Lads in Blue*, published in 1995. A team was formed in the city in 1886 and United came about as an amalgam of two others in 1904, joining the Football League in the 1928/9 season. Since then the team has played at every level and once, in the 1970s, topped the entire Football League for a few days.

The book contains 100-plus pages of chronological history, a biographical chapter on managers, a section on great games, an account of results and an alphabetical 'Who's Who' of all players from 1928 to 1995. There are photographs of virtually every league side and the appendix also has a detailed season-by-season account of all games, results and scorers. The publishers, Yore Books, also produced histories of other 'smaller' football clubs including Newport County, Shrewsbury and Colchester United.

Two good examples of club histories related to athletics and rugby are dealt with in the case studies section, where there is also a reference to the fine history of a Sunderland multi-sport club published in the 1960s. This gives detailed cover of over 150 years of sporting history and is currently being updated.

Two other examples of well-produced and detailed booklets are those published by Castle Cary Cricket Club in Somerset and Alnwick Golf Club in Northumberland. The Castle Cary history is contained in a glossy A4-size booklet packed with information taken from well-researched primary and secondary resource material. It includes interviews with past players and, in the case of the nineteenth century, written accounts of games and players interviewed at the time. This club history goes back to the 1800s and also covers tours made by club members in the late nineteenth and early twentieth centuries as part of the Devon and Somerset Wanderers (including the Olympic trip to Paris). One of these tours was to the Lake District and the Lancashire Coast in 1897. The tour must have been lengthy as they managed to play ten games, winning four, drawing three and losing three.

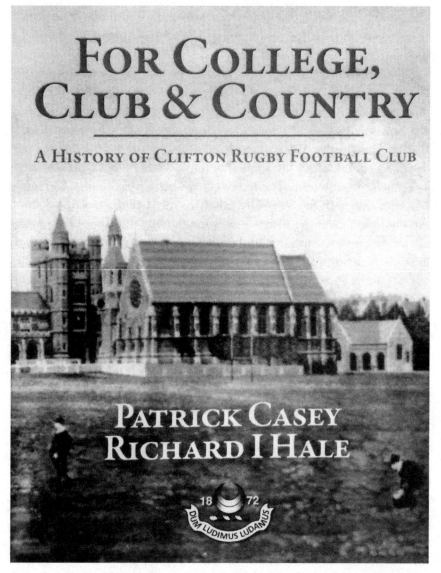

FOR COLLEGE, CLUB & COUNTRY

A HISTORY OF CLIFTON RUGBY FOOTBALL CLUB

PATRICK CASEY
RICHARD I HALE

A useful book dedicated to a club – *For College, Club & Country*. (Author's collection)

This would suggest a tour of ten days at the very least, but it was probably more like a fortnight. It is an indication of the leisure time available to those involved, too. The tour was centred around three hotels: the Keswick Hotel at Keswick, the Old England Hotel at Bowness on Windermere and the Metropolis. A photograph exists of the touring party, probably in the Lake District as the marquee behind the players belongs to a Preston firm.

Alnwick is by no means a large or well-known golf club, yet its history (1907–95) manages to fill ninety tightly packed pages. The written part is accompanied by newspaper cuttings, plans, photographs, scorecards and a detailed map naming and showing the positions of the thirty-six Northumberland golf courses operational during the inter-war years. The grand opening of the course in 1911 is covered in great detail, listing the names and scores of the twenty-six players who made returns in the first competition, and also of those who played and those who did not. Two pages are given to the naming of hundreds of men and women who were members between 1907 and 1913, including Mrs Stone of Shilbottle, Miss Emmerson of the Star Hotel and Miss Leake of the Duchess School. Another page gives the names, professions and photographs of the club's founders: a businessman, a bootmaker, a saddler, an editor, a manager, an auctioneer, a postmaster and two solicitors. The bootmaker, Fred Skelly, appears in the 1901 census age 26, living in Alnwick Market Place with his parents. His father was also a bootmaker.

There are many excellent school histories and most of these can be consulted in local libraries. Both pride in a school and a desire to sell copies of the book often leads to such publications being packed with names and photographs. A good example of such a book is one dedicated to the Pontypridd County School for Boys, which was in operation as such from 1896 to 1973. A number of sports are covered in the book. As might be expected in a Welsh school, rugby was important, although football had a place too. Ironically, the first international to come out of the school, Duncan McGregor, played his rugby for Scotland. That was in the 1906/7 season. A star goalkeeper, William Waters, was praised for his success as an engineering student in the Royal Navy in Edwardian times. He was torpedoed and lost his life in 1914. Cricket is another sport covered in the book with a number of players mentioned in reports on the 1899 season when one Evan Evans was the captain. Tennis also turns up at various stages.

For the family historian the most interesting aspect of such publications is bound to be the photographs as, more often than not, team members are named under the pictures. This is the case with the Pontypridd book, which contains photographs of school rugby teams from the 1920s onwards as well as cricket teams and 'school sprinters'. Particularly successful pupils are also flagged up – pupils such as Iorwerth Isaac and Sydney Jones, who are pictured wearing their Welsh Schools rugby caps in the 1920s.

Another secondary publication worth consulting is the *Oxford Dictionary of National Biography* (*ODNB*) produced at the end of the twentieth century. This dictionary was a complete revamp of the original, which came out a hundred years earlier, and included many people ignored in the first edition as well as twentieth-century updates. Despite the popularity of sport in Victorian times, sportsmen were not placed in the same category as politicians, churchmen and military leaders when it came to recorded history. There are now many sportsmen and women in the *ODNB* and not all of them very famous. Early professional athletes such as Cummings and George are now included, plus many pioneer sportswomen and early British Olympians (the *ODNB* and its regular updates, both contemporary and historical, can also be viewed online).

Modern magazines can also be very useful in helping researchers in their quest for sporting ancestors and especially those magazines dedicated to family history and ones dealing with individual sports. All the leading family history magazines have at one point or another had significant features on the study of sporting ancestors, while occasional letters and case studies can also be of both use and interest. These can be accessed by looking through the indexes of past articles that appear in these magazines from time to time.

A trawl through family history magazines produced in the first decade of the present century produced a few examples of such useful material. In 2004 *Your Family Tree* published a detailed article on footballing ancestors by Newport County supporter, Colin Dean. In another edition of the magazine, the same author wrote about the Slazenger/Schlesinger family and its contribution to the world of tennis. Rosemary Jefferson contributed a piece on bare-knuckle fighter Dick Cain (1819–66). Irish-born and Midlands-bred, Cain was a champion who, like many in his profession, retired into the pub trade.

Family History Monthly featured the beginnings of bare-knuckle fighting in an article by Kim Leslie, which covered an early contest held near Chichester. There has also been a general football ancestry article by expert Ian Nannestad, and a feature on sportsmen appearing on cigarette cards. In the 'Absolute Beginners' section there was once a case study involving a researcher who had discovered both an Edwardian cricketer and an Argentinean rugby player in her family line.

The now defunct *Ancestors* magazine (produced by The National Archives) had lead features on professional boat racing and Olympic cricket. Olympic ancestry is a field that always holds interest and there are usually articles in connection with the topic close to the Olympics themselves. In 2004 *Family History Monthly*'s cover feature was about the tracing of British Olympic ancestry.

Magazines dedicated to modern sport also produce articles with a historical bent, mentioning individuals and, on occasion, totally dedicated themselves to specific sporting figures. This applies to magazines such as *442* for football, *Rugby World* for Rugby Union (which reproduced its first edition on the sport's fiftieth anniversary) and *Running* for athletics. Again it is worth looking at back catalogues and remembering that magazines come and go (and at times merge).

Cricket lends itself particularly to nostalgia articles, as witnessed by examples culled from magazines of the 1980s. In the middle of the decade the then *Wisden Cricket Monthly* ran a series by R.J. Crisp on 'Cricketers Brave', i.e. those who had made their mark while in war service. One in the series was First World War veteran R.C.J. Chichester-Constable. Around the same time, *Cricketer International* ran a series by Alan Gibson with the title 'Cricketers Remembered'. One with the header 'Soldier, Keeper and Captain' was about R.T. Stanyforth (1892–1964) who played for Yorkshire and England. *Cricket World*, no longer in publication, may still prove useful as it covered a wide spectrum of cricket including women's cricket. In 1988 there were regular features on the history of the Bradford leagues and articles on the centenary of the Birmingham and District league and the Craven league. In July of the same year the postbag included a letter in which Tom Iddison of Hartley, Kent wrote about his ancestor Roger, 'the first batsman to score a first-class hundred without hitting a single boundary'. This feat was achieved in 1869.

The October/November 1987 edition of *Northern Runner* had articles on one of the oldest organised races, the Hallam Chase, Sheffield (since 1863), and on historic police sports. *Hockey Field*, dedicated to ladies' hockey, often flagged up histories in its club scene section, too.

Regional magazines such as *Devon Life*, *Lincolnshire Life* and *Down Your Way* (Yorkshire) are also worthy of perusal as, from time to time, they run features on historic sporting events or personalities. In 2004 *Devon Life* published an article on Devon-born and based cricketers. Modern newspapers, especially local ones, are increasingly fond of nostalgia columns. These are now being produced on a regular basis and often feature sporting subjects such as past players connected with local professional sides. Other sports can turn up too. One article on prizefighting in Sussex in the nineteenth century appeared in a family history magazine after first seeing the light of day in the *West Sussex Gazette*.

Academic periodicals are also worth consulting. In recent years sport history has become increasingly accepted among academics and this has led to a serious increase in research and publication. Although the articles can often be based on fairly obscure themes, the evidence in them usually uses individuals as examples or, in some cases, the article can based entirely on the career of a single sportsman or woman. Magazines here include *The International Journal of the History of Sport* and the publications of the British Society of Sport Historians. In the case of the latter, a 1999 newsletter ran articles on Victorian professional running, early sports provision at Cadbury and the birth of speedway. Academic sports historians are usually sports enthusiasts themselves and are willing to discuss sporting individuals, especially if the families have memorabilia or stories, which will add to their own knowledge.

MODERN TECHNOLOGY

The internet has opened up so many possibilities for the family historian and this, naturally, applies to all seeking out sporting ancestors as well. However there is some need for caution. On the positive side, the internet has sped up the collection of evidence beyond the bounds of belief, and the amount of material now available at the push of a button is incredible. On a negative note, much of the material that comes up on the internet has often been processed and reprocessed by others and can at times be a long way from the original source material (which may itself be unreliable). In the case of the internet you 'pays your money and you takes your choice'.

The best way to access useful information remains the faithful search engine. Such is the information in the system that to simply Google a name can come up trumps – especially if the name is an unusual one. Usually the first page of recommended sites provides three or four in which relevant information can be compared and contrasted and which may provide enough solid evidence to start building up a reliable picture.

Better still is the Google Books site, which gives access to digitised copies of original books, magazines and newspapers. This site can be invaluable.

Not only does it present the researcher with a true replica of the original document, it also highlights the name being sought in the search engine and allows access to every reference to that name in the document. If the name being sought is a fairly common one then the field can be cut down by entering into the search engine the name of a sport or sporting venue as well. For example, the entry of the name 'Richard Daft' and the word 'cricket' into the Google Books search engine resulted in many hits, including *Baily's Magazine of Sports and Pastimes,* Vol. 5, published in 1863. Here you are taken directly to a copy of page ninety and to two other references to Richard on the same page. At the top of the page was the information that the book contained four other references to him and these were accessed swiftly.

Google Images can often produce instant success on the pictorial front. Sample trawls for Victorian Aston Villa footballer John Devey and multi-talented sportswoman Lottie Dod produced numerous examples of pictorial evidence, including individual photographs, team photographs, prints, cigarette cards and medals.

There are many family history-specific sites, which are bound to be useful when searching out sporting individuals – some free, some 'pay to use'. Of the free sites, the Latter-day Saints Family Search is one of the most useful if approached with care. Recently revamped and improved, this site gives access to a variety of material worldwide including parish registers, personal family trees and a transcribed 1881 England and Wales census. In terms of the transcription of documents and conclusions drawn from research, the site is littered with errors and often false presumptions, yet it provides enough material to allow progress by process of elimination. It also has one or two interesting 'hidden' features, the best of which perhaps is the ability to access an entire parish register after finding a single entry for that parish in a general list.

Of the paid sites, The Genealogist is one of the most efficient and effective. It leads the researcher swiftly to vital information from the census and civil registration certificates via an extremely clear process of elimination. Early tennis player Spencer Gore (Wimbledon-born) was discovered training as a land agent in Dorset age 21 in 1871 at the touch of a button. Ten years later, married and living in Epsom, Surrey, he was working as a crown receiver and had three young children and four servants. Much of the census evidence for individual sportsmen and women featured in this book was gleaned through this particular site.

In terms of general websites the all-embracing, free for all Wikipedia is a good point to start. Put together by enthusiasts, its reliability is often questioned but the site managers try to ensure that contributors source their evidence and point out circumstances when the facts have not been verified. What the site does do is provide information on a large scale, which can then be tested by visiting other relevant sites.

Another good site, especially when researching sportsmen and women who have enjoyed some form of success in times past, is the educational Spartacus site. The organisers of this site have, in recent years, realised the power of sport as an educational tool and surprisingly detailed biographies can turn up here. Take for example the aforementioned footballer John Devey; Spartacus provides a lengthy page on him packed with photographs, picture cards, written detail and links to other sites for further information. It also includes lengthy quotations on him from modern secondary sources.

As to other useful websites, a representative number are mentioned in the How and Where to Find Resources chapter, and in general it is safe to assume that most major sporting clubs now have their own websites and usually flag up historical sections (see the example of the Clifton Rugby Club in the Case Studies chapter). The same, too, applies to sporting bodies. However, as noted in the following Resources Centres section, these bodies exist mainly to govern the modern sport and officials may not have time to deal with detailed individual queries. In this case, the website may well provide answers or guidance, though these tend to concentrate on immediacy and the kind of information required by students of the modern game.

In most cases, the relevant museum website will prove more useful. For example, the local council in Wrexham has set up a site to back up the ongoing collection of material on Welsh Football in Wrexham Museum (which includes interesting and extraordinary references to a couple of one-armed players).

CDs, though increasingly less popular nowadays, may also prove useful. Every now and then one turns up with a detailed list of past players or something similar. In Scotland, for example, there is a CD available with information on all Scottish League players who played during the second half of the twentieth century.

RESOURCE CENTRES

The best place to start researching sporting ancestry 'on the road' is in a regional archive or local studies library. Not too many years ago this may have read 'county archive' and 'local reference library', but things have changed since, and often for the better. County archives still exist but in many cases they have been moved out of original buildings into newer or redeveloped premises close to museums. Together they form a natural entity known as a 'heritage hub'. Such a move often involves a complete re-cataloguing of material (which is good) and a period when source material is not available to the general public (which is not so good).

The contents of many of these archives and also of The National Archives can be accessed through the comprehensive A2A website. By entering the name of a sport and choosing an archive, you can see what is being held there. For example, entering 'hockey' and 'London Metropolitan Archives' led to a number of photographs of school hockey teams, hospital hockey teams and membership cards, and hockey photographs from personal collections. 'Tennis' and 'Derbyshire Record Office' came up with primary source material relating to Eyam Tennis Club and Belper Lawn Tennis Club; 'polo' and 'Surrey History Centre' a number of documents including Victorian photographs of regimental teams; 'rugby' and 'Gloucestershire Archives' numerous collections of rugby-related material, including autographs, club minutes, school rugby information and much on the Old Patesians Rugby Club. Many sporting clubs have deposited their records in such local archives (rowing clubs seem to have set a particularly good example here – see 'London Metropolitan Archives' and 'rowing club'). There are also some specific local archives which may be worth a visit. The North West Film Archive in Manchester, for example, has early moving pictures of rugby and football matches.

In the case of libraries, most major town and city centre ones have moved on from having local history sections to fully blown and separate local studies centres. The growth of interest in family history during the last quarter of the twentieth century is a major reason for this development. A good example of what might turn up in a library was provided in a British Society of Sports Historians' newsletter in 1999 with a detailed account of sporting material in Warrington Public Library, Cheshire. Twenty sports in all were covered (including angling, darts and chess, which do not feature in this book). The library held the minutes of the local council, of its

A valuable letter on rugby (England vs Scotland, 1901) from Edgar 'Tegger' Elliot.
(KG archivist)

He played cricket, too: Edgar Elliot, *c.* 1903. (KG archivist)

gymnasium committee (1896–1935) and town hall, parks and baths committee (1872–74). Its local collection also contained various other minute books, accounts, annual reports, photographs and yearbooks, as well as handbooks, rulebooks, fixture lists, programmes, cuttings and leaflets from the 1850s onwards. It is difficult to say whether this is typical or not, but it does give some idea of the type of material that might turn up.

The British Library's site at Colindale keeps copies of virtually every newspaper, local and national, as well as some vintage football programmes. It is well worth checking for newspapers that cannot be found in a local archive, as well as sporting papers such as *Bell's Sporting Chronicle*. Material relating to Scottish football clubs and other football-related periodicals can also be found here.

One of the most interesting and mysterious of archives is the club archive. Here it is really a case of pot luck. Sporting clubs large and small have developed their own attitudes to archival material over the years. Some have shown no interest at all while others have carefully maintained their archives and have a nominated person to look after them. Some will have kept evidence of sporting activity but have yet to sort it, while others may have put all their historical material into a local archive. A letter, email or telephone call to a club with ancestral connections will quickly sort out the particular situation there. There are few clubs without at least one member enthusiastic about its history, and it is likely that you may be pointed in his or her direction with every chance of a successful outcome.

In terms of the type of evidence likely to turn up in a sport club archive, the case study on Sunderland's Ashbrooke Sports Club should prove helpful. In general, photographic evidence is popular with sports clubs (and schools) and many have historic pictures adorning their walls, in most cases the names of team members are given beneath them. Clubs are also apt to produce their own club histories from time to time and it can often be the older ones that prove most useful to the family historian. Other notable material that has turned up in club archives includes programmes, committee meeting minute books (including team selections), cuttings books, correspondence and member's obituaries.

Museums are also worth a visit, and not merely in order to get a flavour of a sport in which an ancestor might have been involved. Some of the material on display may be in written form and a friendly curator might be persuaded to open a case and allow access to such material. Many general museums have sport-specific displays, even though they might only consist of a glass case or two. This is particularly true where the city or town in which the museum is placed has a professional sporting side or a reputation for a particular sport. The Dock Museum at Barrow-in-Furness, for example, has displays on its local Rugby League side and its halcyon days in the middle of the twentieth century; also on its football team, which was once in the major leagues. Wrexham Library, revamped in 2010, has the earliest moving picture of an international football match (Wales vs Ireland 1906), while Wrexham Museum, as noted above, is constantly building on its important – if relatively new – collection of material relating to Welsh football.

Perhaps the most useful museum for ancestral sporting research purposes will be the sports-specific one and, despite hard times economically, there seem to be an ever-growing number of these. England has its National Football Museum at Preston. The Scottish National Football Musuem is at Hampden Park; suitably, as it is the home of Scottish football. Cricket has an MCC Museum at Lord's and rugby a state-of-the-art museum at Twickenham, which includes remarkable moving pictures from the early twentieth century. Newmarket has the National Horse Racing Museum, while Henley on Thames has a museum dedicated to the river and rowing. Brooklands deal with early motor racing and there are also museums dedicated to golf (at St Andrews), archery (The Dick Galloway Archery Museum) and cycling (The National Cycle Collection). Wimbledon, naturally, is the place for tennis memorabilia.

Many of these museums also have useful and easy to use websites. This is particularly true of the National Horse Racing Museum and the Amateur Boxing Association (ABA), which are both very strong on records and pen pictures of past performers (in the case of racing, both human and animal).

As an example of the usefulness of such centres, the football museums may have detailed information on player registrations, though indications are that the sorting out of this is still a work in progress. Often, too, the museum or collection of memorabilia is in the same place as the headquarters of the particular sporting body (although this is not always the case). Such sporting bodies often have archives of their own, but it is wise to make general enquiries first. The main aim of these sporting bodies is to govern the modern sport and the history is often an afterthought. Letters and queries may remain unanswered unless directed to the right person, if indeed there is a 'right person'.

It is in such places that the most fascinating and unpredictable evidence may turn up – material such as the Droitwich Brine Baths Visitors Book

(1887–99), which contains the names and addresses of many sportsmen, sportswomen and teams that came there to exercise. These include the Aston Villa Football team prior to a Victorian FA Cup Final, and Herbert Laurie of Bank, Worcester, who was a well-known amateur athlete who used the facilities between 1889 and 1890.

Tennis ladies from the 1920s, found in the Ashbrooke Archives. (KG archivist)

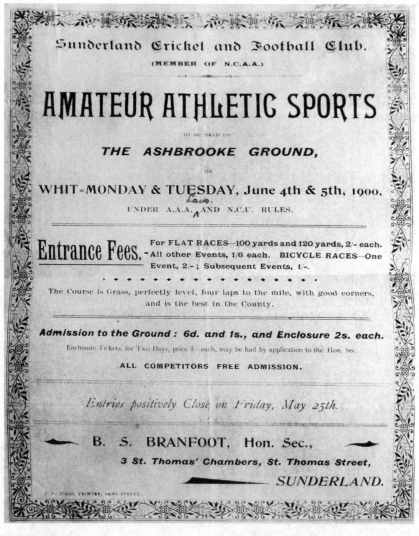

Victorian Whitsuntide Sports. (KG archivist)

CASE STUDIES

CASE STUDY ONE: THE ARCHIVES OF ASHBROOKE SPORTS CLUB, SUNDERLAND, TYNE AND WEAR (FORMERLY COUNTY DURHAM)

The amount of historical sporting material in the possession of Ashbrooke Sports Club is in many ways unique, so much so that the editors of the Tyne and Wear volume in English Heritage's *Played in Britain* series flagged up this archive for special consideration. The club has bowls, cricket, hockey, rugby, squash and tennis sections that have adopted the Sunderland name for each sport (Sunderland RFC, Sunderland CC, etc.). It has existed in its present premises in the Ashbrooke area of Sunderland since its rugby and cricket sections took place there in May 1887. Both of these sections existed separately before that date as Sunderland Cricket Club and Sunderland Football (or Foot-ball Club), which explains why some of the archival records take us much further back in the nineteenth century. Athletics, cycling, baseball and soccer have also featured strongly in the club's history and they too show up in the archival material.

In each of the examples given below, the primary or secondary nature of the source material is pointed out (see How and Where to Find Resources) as well as the actual date, whether the evidence is written or pictorial, the nature of the evidence and the sport involved. There is then a brief description of the material and an explanation of how it might be useful to anyone studying their sporting ancestors. This overview gives the reader an idea of the type of material that can still turn up in such an archive. The list is in date order and includes the archival reference as an example of the kind of referencing used in archival work. In this referencing the 'A' stands for Ashbrooke and the next letter usually for the relevant sport; the number was allotted to ensure quick retrieval of the relevant piece.

Cricket minute book, 1857–62 (A/C 7) – primary/written

This is a small, paperback, handwritten book covering the earlier years of Sunderland Cricket Club. It lists team and club members as well as details of games played.

Cricket photograph, 1869 (A/P/CO 1) – primary/pictorial

Two separate photographs in the archives relate to an against-the-odds cricket game – one is of Parr's professional England side and this one is of the XXII local men who played them. The players are named, though not all were regulars for the local cricket team. The game was to raise funds for Sunderland Infirmary.

Tennis notebook, 1885–86 (A/T 5) – primary/written

A slim notebook relating to Sunderland Tennis Club just before Ashbrooke opened. Both males and females played and the book contains many names and addresses, including female ancestral relatives of the author of this book.

Athletics and cycling ledger, 1893–1904 and 1910 (A/O 3) – primary/written

A huge ledger with a programme relating to the annual Whitsuntide Athletics Meeting. The names, addresses and clubs of entrants for all events are noted in here, running to hundreds for each one: a real gold mine of information for both the social and family historian.

Tennis photograph, *c.* 1906 (A/P/T 1) – primary/pictorial

Early photographs of ladies playing sport are to be valued and there are many in this archive, including those of cricket and tennis. This particular shot shows the successful ladies side that did well on the national circuit. It portrays the Aitcheson sisters, one of whom succeeded at Wimbledon and in the early modern Olympics.

Rugby newspaper cutting, 1910 (A/R 12) – primary/written
A good example of an interesting primary source where a participant
looks back at an event; in this case the rugby club's victory in the very first
county cup in 1881.

Hockey photograph, 1912 (to index) – primary/pictorial
For some reason the hockey archive is rather thin, but this photograph
is included here because it depicts a member of the Sunderland hockey
club, Cecil Tindell Green, in an England side (he gained seven caps). The
photograph was a recent discovery made along with other pictures in an
old suitcase.

Cricket and rugby scorebook, 1930 (A/C 4) – primary/written
There are dozens of scorebooks in the cricket archive covering everything
from first team to friendlies and packed with names. This one contains the
teams who played in a friendly game of cricket between the rugby club and
their 'ladies'.

Bowls cartoon, 1936 (A/P/B 4) – primary/pictorial
Cartoons of sporting personalities were very popular with the local press
during the middle of the twentieth century and it is possible to come across
caricatures of whole teams. This one is of the bowls team, which won a
national newspaper trophy.

**Baseball programme, 1937 (box file) – primary/written and
pictorial**
A single game of baseball was played to celebrate the coronation of George
VI, but some wise club member at the time decided to keep all the doc-
umentation relating to it in a file. The file contains correspondence, law
books, photographs, posters and programmes. The game was between the
Yorkshire league and the Canadian national side.

**General sports history book, 1963 (library) – secondary/written
and pictorial**
To Ashbrooke and Beyond 1887–1962 was published in 1963 and produced
by a group of efficient and hardworking researchers. It is full of names and
information on people who have played in all sports at the club.

Football file, mainly 1980s (A/S 1) – secondary/written and pictorial

Sunderland AFC, a premiership football side in 2010, played on a field on the Ashbrooke site in 1881/2. The club has collected articles and correspondence on this and there is a file for consultation. At this time many of the players were young schoolteachers.

The Lansdown Complex in Dublin has a similar Victorian sporting pedigree; archery, croquet, lawn tennis, rugby and cricket were all played there on a regular basis. The complex also had a cinder track used for athletics.

Case Study Two: My Family and Sport

The aim of this case study is to persuade, firstly, that it is important to gather in past memorabilia from the family and, secondly, that it is wise to keep current records for the sake of future family historians. We all bemoan missed opportunities in our family history research and can put this right for our own descendants by keeping current personal records in order.

The author's maternal grandfather (front row, dark shorts) in the victorious Barrow Post Office Wednesday league side, 1920s. (Author's collection)

My maternal grandfather Fred 'Pop' Stephens (1886–1952) was a keen amateur sportsman all his life. As a young unmarried man (he did not wed until his 30s) he played football and cricket. This was in the Edwardian period when Church and sport went hand in hand. His family, Cumbrian but of Cornish descent, was strong on Methodism and he participated in both sports in the local Church leagues. We have medals and photographs from this time.

During the First World War he sent a letter home to his mother, which noted that he had won a cross-country run and was going to receive 'some fags' as a prize. His brother, Charles, kept a detailed diary during the same war. He was in India. Here, when the anticipated trouble failed to material-ise, sporting activity became an essential feature of daily life in the army and his writings tell of football, cricket and tennis leagues, mostly organised by the YMCA.

In the 1920s Fred played football for the local Post Office side in one of the popular Wednesday leagues set up for fitness and pleasure during the half-day holiday. We have photographs of a number of his teams. For a couple of seasons my paternal grandfather, a postman, played in goal for the same side. Unfortunately we do not have a picture of them together.

The author's father (front row, goalkeeper) with the Royal Signals Unit football side, Sicily, 1944. (Author's collection)

My father, Rex Gregson (1920–94), was also a keen amateur sports-man. He always claimed that he was a good cricketer at school and was proud when he managed to lay his hands on a couple of old school maga-zines from the 1930s that proved that he had enjoyed success both in cricket and athletics. During the Second World War he was in the Signals in the Middle East and Italy. His diary refers to numerous inter-regi-mental football matches and a couple of disastrous forays against strong Palestinian sides.

While in Sicily he played in goal for the Signals and was called up to rep-resent the army in three games against Italian professional side Reggiana on the mainland after the Italian surrender. The army side was packed with professionals and included a pre-war England international. The profes-sional goalkeeper was sent home on compassionate leave and my father was invited to join the side. In the three games played he did not concede a single goal and was extremely proud of this. Late in life he followed up members of the side and put together a file, which includes programmes, photographs, newspaper articles and correspondence. These three games were important to football history as they were connected, through a member of the Reggiana team, to the later move of English footballers to Italy and also the formation of the Anglo/Italian league and cup.

After the war my father played local league cricket, football and table tennis and we have numerous photographs. My mother played representa-tive hockey at school but we have been unable to trace any records so far.

I was born in 1948, played cricket, rugby and football at a low level at school and university and have kept evidence from school magazines and university newspapers. In my 30s I was sucked into the fun-run boom started by the Great North Run and the London Marathon. I managed nineteen of the former and three of the latter before wear and tear set in. I have scrapbooks, certificates, medals, photographs, programmes, newspaper accounts and a video recording to pass on.

My three sons (b. 1979, 1984 and 1986) continue to enjoy sporting suc-cess. The eldest has won golf competitions, the middle (prematurely retired through injury) coached Rugby Union and the youngest is involved in mixed martial arts at a semi-professional level. All three played cricket, rugby and football at school, for clubs and, in some cases, representatively. One captained a county schools rugby team containing current England internationals, while another played the same sport for north of England schools and American football for Great Britain.

We have medals, cups, trophies and files with programmes, photographs, newspaper cuttings, correspondence and school magazines, which we hope to keep in the family. We also have a photograph of my wife in her school hockey team.

Two of the author's sons in Leeds Celtics American football team, 2006. (Author's collection)

A man of mystery (rugby or football player, may have only one eye) found among ancestral photographs, Barrow-in-Furness, *c.* 1890–95. (Author's collection)

CASE STUDY THREE: TWO CLUB HISTORIES

Although club histories vary greatly in quality, many of them have been well researched and invariably mention as many names as possible. This is a good sales ploy – as is the inclusion of numerous team photographs accompanied by the names of team members. A couple of examples of good club histories should serve as indicators of what to look out for.

Running in the Pools is a 100-page, A4-size booklet produced by schoolteacher, athletics coach and former distance runner Ken Lupton. It is a thorough history of West Hartlepool's (and after its renaming in the 1960s, Hartlepool's) Burn Road Harriers up to the club centenary in 1995. The book begins with a number of photocopied extracts from newspapers in the year of foundation, 1895, and the very first page mentions over twenty original club members. Of Bill Crick, a founder member, the author of the booklet writes:

> Joining as a young man aged 19 years, W B Crick was to be an early club captain and winner of the Patrons Cup in 1897 and again in 1903. For many years he was club trainer. His service to the club was recognised with the presentation of a fine mantle clock when he retired from that position in 1932. Born in 1876, he died in 1952 at the age of 76.

There are also copies of programmes from sports meetings held across the region and a fascinating photograph of nine lady athletes in 1922. The Hendry family apparently boasted a family full of athletes at this time: five females and four males. One of the founders of the Harriers, railwayman William Lee, had a son called Jack who moved to Newcastle in his 20s, joined Heaton Harriers and represented Great Britain in the 1908 Olympics. Dick Ripley was also a fine runner and there is a photograph of him in a 4 x 440yds relay team alongside the legendary Eric Liddell, whose Olympic exploits were featured in the film *Chariots of Fire*.

The historical part of the Bristol Clifton Rugby Football Club website is a fine example of a resource useful to family historians. The club was founded in 1872 and thus has a lengthy history. Its website is divided into decades and has areas dedicated to the founders, famous players, famous matches, grounds and the war memorial.

The pages given over to Edwin Field (1871–1947), a Clifton player in his youth who moved on to play for Cambridge University, Middlesex

Wanderers, Barbarians and England, gives an idea of what to expect. There are details of his representative record and pictures of him in his England kit. There are photographs of him at Clifton College, in which others are named with him. There are pictures, too, of his Cambridge University cricket and rugby sides and the England team that played Wales in 1893 (including Dick Lockwood who features in The Amateurs chapter). There are details of his family, both as a youth and after marriage, and references to his obituary in *The Times* newspaper.

The war memorial section of this website covers both world wars of the twentieth century and gives an index of names of over forty men connected to the club who died in the First World War. This in turn gives access to pages of information on the people involved. These are admirably thorough, as in the case of Francis John Hannan, a Bristol-born man killed in action on 5 July 1916. The site covers not only his war record but his sporting record too, and has numerous extracts from local newspapers as well as official reports and letters relating to the action in which he was killed. There are photographs of him in uniform and in sports teams, plus photographs of his family home. There is also a picture and details of his wife, Edith Hannam (née Boucher), who won tennis medals under her married name at the 1912 Olympics, and a note to the effect that her brothers played rugby for Clifton (there is even a team photograph with her husband and brother standing side by side).

The Clifton website is not the only way of accessing material on those who played for this ancient club. A 300-page book was published in 2009, *For College, Club & Country*, which is packed with detailed information, both written and pictorial. Though Clifton Rugby Club has made a special effort in producing their website, it does give encouragement to researchers to find out if their ancestral clubs have done anything similar.

CASE STUDY FOUR: WOMEN IN SPORT

Family historians tend to find it easier to discover more information about their male ancestors than their female ones. This is a sad and often frustrating fact of life, reflecting that it was mostly men who wrote the records and the histories in the past. In the case of sporting history, however, not all is doom and gloom. The explosion of popular sport in the Victorian and Edwardian periods produced a number of sports played by ladies, and where this was the case there are likely to be records. Three sportswomen successful during the Victorian and Edwardian eras make for good case studies: Lottie Dod (1871–1960), Lily Gower (1877–1959) and Madge Syers (1881–1917). It is noteworthy that they played as amateurs and two of them lived well into living memory.

Lottie Dod was a multi-talented sportswoman from Bebington, Cheshire. At the time of the 1881 census young Lottie was living with her widowed mother, who was described as a housekeeper. The family was still wealthy enough to be able to afford both a cook and a housemaid. In general, many of the successful sportswomen from this period came from homes able to support them in playing sport. Lottie's first success came in tennis at the age of 15. She won the Wimbledon ladies' title in 1887, taking the final with the loss of only two games. Three years later, while still in her teens, she contributed a fascinating article on tennis to the Badminton Library series. Of special interest is her attitude to dress codes (too restrictive), male attitudes to female tennis players (too pompous) and the attitudes of other sportswomen to men and their own sporting achievements (too coy).

Still in her 20s, and by now five times Wimbledon champion, Lottie stopped playing competitive tennis. In 1889 she was selected to play hockey for England. In 1904 she won the women's amateur golf championship and four years later rounded off a most successful sporting career with a silver medal in archery at the 1908 London Olympics (her brother Willie took gold in the same sport at the same Games). She was also adept at winter sports and was one of the first females to go down the Cresta Run.

Lily Gower was born Lilias Mary Gower, the daughter of a wealthy English magistrate and his Scottish wife. Lily was born in Scotland but raised in Wales. She was an expert croquet player and won her first singles tournament while in her early 20s. Having enjoyed success in women's competitions, she began entering men's open competitions and, in 1901, won the Open Gold Medal – despite being accused (controversially) of cheating in the semi-finals. She won the Open Championship on two further occasions, a feat shared to date by only two other females. She was also, due to confusion with the rules, once winner of the men's Gold Medal. She married in 1902 and became Mrs Beaton. There have been articles and booklets on her and her name appears on a number of ancestral websites.

Madge Syers was quite a character. She was born Florence Margaret Cave in London and became a successful ice skater – particularly after she married coach Edgar Syers, who was more than twice her age at the time of marriage (1899). She became the first world and Olympic female figure skating champion and, like Lily Gower, shocked the sporting world by taking on the men. She entered the world championship in 1902 and won a silver medal. At the time this was considered a male-only sport, though there was no official rule banning women. According to a contemporary tale, Salchow, the winner, offered her his medal, claiming she was the better skater. Women were then banned from the contest as the movements of their feet and ankles during performance could not be seen beneath their long skirts, and so could not be properly judged.

In Great Britain, however, an open championship was set up in 1903. Syers entered and won while her husband took second place. She won it again in 1904 and in 1906 became the first women's world champion. In 1908 at the London Summer Olympics she took gold in the women's figure skating and bronze with her husband in the pairs. She did not enjoy robust health and retired soon after the Olympics. She was also a good swimmer and horsewoman.

[June 2, 1866.]　　　PUNCH. OR THE LONDON CHARIVARI.　　　237

BOAT-RACE OF THE FUTURE.—DRIFTING DOWN TO THE STARTING-POINT.

Ladies take up organised sport in *Punch* (2 June 1866 compendium). (Author's collection)

Though it could be argued that the case studies of these ladies might only be of real interest to their comparatively few descendants (and Lottie never married), they do provide a number of general points. Lottie Dod was involved in sports where, as individual chapters have shown, female participation was the order of the day: tennis, hockey, golf and archery. Her success at the Olympics also exposes the myth that female involvement did not enter the Games until well into the twentieth century.

Possible name confusion is apparent in the other two cases. Lily Gower is a well-known name in croquet history; Mrs Lily Beaton less so. In reverse, Mrs Syers was a star ice skater while Miss Florence Cave has left little in the way of reputation. Such name changes need to be held in mind when researching personal ancestry. Victorian attitudes towards women in sport may also be of interest and can often be seen in the cartoons published in magazines such as *Punch*, particularly during the mid-Victorian period.

CASE STUDY FIVE: EARLY LINCOLNSHIRE OLYMPIANS

As noted in the main text, local and regional magazines often feature lesser-known successful athletes and Olympians, in particular, tend to surface around the time of a current Olympics. Take Lincolnshire for example. Harold Wilson, born at Horncastle in January 1885, was a middle distance runner, specialising over the 1500m distance. His chance for Olympic success came at the White City in London in 1908.

Wilson was on good form in the approach to these London Games and recorded a world-record time in his favourite distance during the Olympic trials. Unfortunately he fell a little short in the actual event, ending up with silver medal and only a couple of metres behind the USA's Mike Shepherd. He did, however, gain gold for his role in the team that participated in the now discontinued 3 mile team event. This took the form more associated with modern cross-country running. Points were awarded for positions in the individual 3 mile race and the team with the lowest count given first place. Here Harold Wilson proved his worth. He was racing well beyond his preferred distance and finished in fifth place. This was said at the time to have been pivotal to Britain securing the gold medal.

Little more is known about Wilson. He later left the country to work as a professional runner in Canada and South Africa. He died, just turned 30, in

1916 and it is reasonable to assume that there may be a connection between his death and the First World War. Finding the truth may not be easy as records reveal that, sadly, a large number of men called Harold or Harry Wilson lost their lives in action during that darkest year of that war.

An early Olympic tennis champion with Lincolnshire connections was solicitor Charles Dixon, born in Grantham in February 1873. Dixon enjoyed an extraordinarily successful Olympic career. In 1908, while Harold Wilson was gaining his two medals on the track, Dixon was securing a bronze in the men's doubles. Four years later, the Games moved to Stockholm and the Lincolnshire tennis star returned with three medals – a gold in the mixed indoor doubles, a silver in the men's indoor singles and a bronze in the men's indoor doubles. His brother, John, was a well-known first-class cricketer.

Perhaps the best known of the early Lincolnshire Olympians is David Cecil, Lord Burleigh. A member of a historically famous family, he was born in 1905 near Stamford, attended Eton and Cambridge, and formed the basis for one of the characters in the successful feature film *Chariots of Fire*. He took gold in the 400m hurdles at the 1928 Olympics and enjoyed success at other Olympic and Commonwealth events. In later life he became involved in politics and athletics administration. He died in 1981.

CASE STUDY SIX: A FAMILY AT SPORT

Few people can claim to be part of a 'very sporting family', but such families do exist and are worth pursuing. Take the modern Mancunian Neville family in the late twentieth century, where two sons were football internationals and a daughter represented the country at netball. One of these sons (Phil) was also an accomplished cricketer and could have followed a first-class cricketing career. There are also examples of sporting families from earlier times – one of the best being the Worcestershire Foster family, who even have a website dedicated to it that tells the story in vivid detail.

The father of the family, Henry, a Sussex-born minister, became house-master at the newly-founded Malvern College in 1867 and remained there for almost half a century. He was a scratch golfer who had excelled at sports when at school and university; including cricket, rowing, fives and archery. He and his wife Sophie had ten children surviving infancy, seven boys and three girls. The girls were sports-orientated and good at cricket. Cicely, the youngest of the three, played golf for England.

The boys excelled at a variety of sports, notably cricket, football, golf and racquets. Harry (b. 1873) won numerous national racquets champion-ships. Bill (b. 1874) won the racquets pairs at Queen's. Reginald or 'Tip' (b. 1878) was a racquets champion, captained England at cricket and played football for his country seven times. Basil (b. 1882) was a national racquets champion. Geoff (b. 1884) won competitions at racquets, fives and golf, and played football for England as an amateur twice. Maurice (b. 1889) captained Worcestershire at cricket and won championships at fives and rac-quets. Johnnie (b. 1890) was a championship winner at racquets and played football for the Corinthians and cricket for Worcestershire. Three brothers captained Worcestershire at cricket and five of them scored more than one first-class century. It is little wonder that, for many years, Worcestershire was humorously known as 'Fostershire' and, with the three girls and the father, the Fosters were able to field a formidable cricket side.

An equally interesting family is the Daft family from Nottingham. Brothers Charles (1830–1915) and Richard (1835–1900) both played cricket for Nottinghamshire and Charles later turned his hand to outfitting crick-eters (1881 census). Richard's two sons Harry (1866–1945) and Richard (1863–1934) also turned out for Nottinghamshire. Harry played football for Notts County, Nottingham Forest and England and also had national lacrosse trials for his country. Charles' son – also Charles (see The Amateurs chapter) – was a footballer and won the national amateur hurdles title.

Although the Fosters were a 'one-off', there have been a number of fami-lies as successful as the Dafts from Victorian times onwards and, as noted in the introduction to this book, sport is often 'in the genes'.

CASE STUDY SEVEN: A MODEL ANCESTRAL STUDY

The role of the newspaper as a research tool is featured in How and Where to Find Resources. Researcher David Robarts' study of a direct sporting ances-tor provides a good example of the successful use of newspaper in research. His ancestor was prominent in what was, at the time, a minority sport. David's researches provide a good model for others to follow and further results can be viewed on his website: www.stepneyrobarts.co.uk/41.htm.

The ancestor concerned was Captain Gerald (Timmy) Robarts (1878–1961). Educated at Eton and Magdalen College, Oxford, he joined the seventh Hussars in 1899, saw action in the Boer War 1901–02 and also served with distinction during the First World War. In 1881 and 1891 he was living in his native place, Lillingstone Dayrell in Buckinghamshire. In 1901 he was an officer student living in barracks in Kent, and in 1905 he married.

Captain Robarts was a successful cricketer, but it was on the squash court that he really excelled. This was in the early 1920s when squash was a minority game, dominated by military men, with a number of them quite elderly in sporting terms. Patient research has led to the discovery of well over twenty separate references to Robarts' squash activities in *The Times* newspaper between 1923 and 1926. The captain was then in his mid- to late 40s. In these reports, David Robarts picked up his ancestor's links to the Bath Club and his involvement in contests against members of other clubs (including Queen's and the RAC). One of Captain Robarts' opponents, representing the MCC, was H.D.G. Leveson-Gower. Leveson-Gower was a well-known figure in cricketing circles who, for many years, had his own touring side packed with successful professional and amateur cricketers. Correspondents also noted, on a number of occasions, that Captain Robarts had 'a squash court of his own'. The true value of Captain Robarts' story as a case study lies in noting the quality and quantity of information gathered from the newspaper report. This speaks for itself:

Boston, Feb 24 - Captain Gerald Robarts has won the American Squash Rackets Championship, beating Mr W. Harrity in the final round - Reuters.

(*The Times*, 26 February 1924)

THE BATH CLUB CUP

The play of Captain Gerald Robarts, the winner of the American Championship, was of great interest yesterday. Captain Robarts in the American and Canadian tour made the astonishing effort of playing 17 matches in 19 days and winning all of them. Sometimes he played two matches in one day. When he was not playing a match he appears to have been dressing, undressing, or packing. Occasionally he seems to have slept, and sometimes, one must presume, have eaten.

(*The Times*, 6 March 1924)

He also played against the doyen of early squash featured in the main text:

AMATEUR CHAMPIONSHIP

The best match of the day, and that which may decide the Championship, was played between Captain J. E. Tomkinson and Captain Gerald Robarts. Captain Tomkinson was once a very great player. He is not so good as he was at one time. For this reason he has trained, and he won the third game against Captain Robarts by being the faster and less exhausted player in the court. Captain Tomkinson won by two games to one (15 – 7, 6 – 15, 15 – 4).

(*The Times*, 9 December 1924)

AMATEUR CHAMPIONSHIP

The Amateur Squash Rackets Championship (holder Captain V.A. Cazalet) was begun in the Bath Club courts yesterday. The Prince of Wales has entered for the competition, as also have all the best of the British squash rackets players, with the exception of Captain T.O. Jameson, Captain Gerald Robarts, and Mr S.M. Toyne'.

(*The Times*, 14 December 1926)

Justifiably proud of his ancestor's sporting achievement (and his own research), David Robarts ends the sporting section of his online family history thus:

In 1924 he went to New York on the SS Tyrrhenia from Liverpool, aged forty-six, to take part in a squash tournament which, somewhat typically for the USA, was described as the world championship even though only the USA, Canada and Great Britain were involved. To be fair perhaps no other countries played squash in 1924 and, that said, he won the contest so can be regarded as the squash Olympian of his time at the age of 46. Pretty impressive.

CASE STUDY EIGHT: MYSTERY SPORTING PERSONALITIES

One of the most interesting aspects of researching sporting ancestry is the very real possibility that an ancestor might have been a sporting success and that very little was written about it at the time. Today, thanks to the global media and extended leisure time, sport is all consuming – and that applies to nearly every sport. This was not the case in the past. Take, for example, the twenty-four men who competed in Olympics single cricket match at Paris in 1900.

Just before the First World War, when the issue of Olympic medals was being sorted out retrospectively, the two teams of twelve who played in the only Olympic cricket match were awarded gold and silver medals – the English (representing Britain) gained the gold and the French the silver. Thanks to recent research, we know a little about the ordinary Englishmen from Devon and Somerset who took the gold but virtually nothing about the French who took the silver. Indeed the French may be of interest to English family history researchers as nearly all of them had British surnames and were, we suspect, employees at the British Embassy or British business-men working in France. Unfortunately, in most cases we have surnames alone, although in some cases there are initials as well. There may, therefore, be people living in Britain today with British sporting ancestors who won silver Olympic medals when representing France at cricket!

In the course of this book being written, many successful sportsmen and sportswomen have turned up about whom very little seems to be known. In some cases the information on them appears to have come from one source alone and was simply repeated. Equally frustrating is the Victorian's tendency to give a mere initial instead of providing a full Christian name. This was true with sportswomen in particular, as in the case of the croquet genius Miss K. Philbrick who was national champion in 1876, 1877, 1881 and 1882.

One problem in trying to find out more about the elusive Miss Philbrick is that croquet had a hiatus soon after her victories and fell out of favour for more than a decade. All early croquet records online give her initial alone, thus making necessary some more general family tree sleuthing. Using all the machinery of the Latter-day Saints and The Genealogist websites nar-rows down the field considerably. She must have been unmarried around the time of the 1881 census as she won the titles under her maiden name, and the surname Philbrick and the female initial 'K' (Katherine/Kathleen?) was not a common one. After eliminating the too young and the too old (and taking into account that croquet could be played quite late in life), one candidate alone stands out.

Katherine, or Catherine Ludlam Philbrick, was born at Louth in Lincolnshire in 1844. She was the daughter of an Essex-born doctor of medicine (MD) and in 1851 she was in Louth with the family. They had moved to Warwickshire by 1861 and then to on to Brighton, where she appears still 'at home' and unmarried in 1871 age 26 and 1881 age 36. No indication of any occupation is given in the relevant census returns.

Is this our Miss K. Philbrick? She seems a good candidate, belonging to the right class for the sport and still unmarried and in her 30s. There remains a problem, however. On all official records except the 1861 census she is Catherine with a 'C'. Not to be outdone, the author would argue that she may have gone for the sporting 'Kate' at an early age, which might explain the initial. Then again, there may be those out there who know different and can solve the mystery of croquet's Miss K. Philbrick once and for all.

How and Where to Find Resources

N.B. Comments have been included only in cases where the resource or resource centre is well known to the author.

General Family History

Combined use of these two sites can lead to the swift discovery of nine-teenth-century and early twentieth-century ancestors:

www.familysearch.org – a free site set up by members of the Church of Jesus Christ of the Latter-day Saints, it offers two different search engines.

www.thegenealogist.co.uk – a well-established 'pay to use' site with a search engine geared to the quick discovery of the ancestor being sought.

General Sporting History

Bevan, Alun Wynn (ed.), *Welsh Sporting Greats* (Ceredigion, 2001) – deals mainly with late twentieth-century sporting personalities with one or two from earlier times.

Grayson, Edward, *Corinthians and Cricketers* (London, 1957) – an essential work on the history of amateur cricket and football, naming many names.

Huggins, Mike, *The Victorians and Sport* (London, 2004) – recognised as a key study of the topic. This book also has a useful list of relevant contemporary sporting magazines and newspapers, and acts as a gateway to many other useful sources.

Makepeace, Christopher, *Lancashire in the 20's and 30's from Old Photographs* (London, 1977) – an example of the type of photographic collection that often contains sports-related photographs.

Mor O'Brien, A., *The County School for Boys Pontypridd 1896–1973* (Pontypridd, 1989) – what to expect on the sporting front from a good school history.

Moses, E. W. et al, *To Ashbrooke and Beyond* (Sunderland, 1963) – all that the history of a multi-sport club should be and filled with information on individual sportsmen and women.

Norridge, Julian, *Can We Have Our Balls Back, Please? How The British invented Sport* (London, 2008) – very good on the early days of many sports with an extremely useful bibliography.

Palmer, Roy; Raven, Jon, *The Rigs of the Fair: Popular Sports and Pastimes in the Nineteenth Century Through Songs, Ballads and Contemporary* (Cambridge, 1976) – a good selection of songs and ballads referencing individuals. Further examples of sports-related songs and ballads can be found in other books by Roy Palmer and there are many ballads on Tyneside boat racing in collections of Tyneside songs from the Victorian period (look for songs by Joe Wilson, Ned Corvan and 'Geordie' Ridley).

Richardson, Michael, *Durham City from Old Photographs* (Stroud, 2009) – another example of sporting photographs in a local context.

Sampson Low, Marston and Co, *Encyclopaedia of Sport* (London/Great Missenden, 1959) – packed with sporting names and details. This firm was also responsible for the publication of *The Hardy Boys* and *Nancy Drew Mysteries*.

Tames, Richard, *The Victorian and Edwardian Sportsman* (Princes Risborough, 2007) – although only a booklet, it is very informative on sports and sportsmen in the late nineteenth century and early twentieth century.

Wilkinson, Jennifer, 'Absolute Beginners: Work in Progress', *Family History Monthly*, No. 183 (July 2010) – a sporting family tree including an Edwardian cricketer and an Argentinean polo player.

Boy's Own Newspaper (weekly 1879–1913, thereafter monthly until 1967, also bound annuals) – a surprising amount of information on all forms of sport from school to professional.

'Holy Smoke', *Family History Monthly*, No. 155 (April 2008) – an article dealing with the history of cigarette cards.

Oxford Dictionary of National Biography – also available online and regularly updated, it has an ever-increasing number of sporting personalities.

Played in Manchester (2004), *Played in Birmingham* (2006), *Played in Liverpool* (2007) and *Played in Tyne and Wear* (2010) from the *Played in Britain* Series (English Heritage Books) – very detailed, thoroughly researched and packed with photographs, many of them archival. Also leaves no stone unturned in examining every aspect of sporting activity in the locality. An excellent starting point for the family historian.

Steering the Sailors' Life and Lighting the Sailors' Way: 1856–1906 (*c.* 1906) – this little book on the history of seamen's missions has a number of sports-related photographs.

The Badminton Library of Sports and Pastimes (London and Boston, 1885–1902) – over thirty volumes dealing in detail with individual sports and often written by active sportsmen and women. Some of these are referred to under individual sports below.

The British Library Newspaper Library, Colindale Avenue, London, NW9 5HU – known simply as 'Colindale', the place to go when looking for newspaper evidence, as well as other forms of printed sporting memorabilia. For indexes: www.bl.uk/collections and www.bl.uk/newspapers (special arrangements may be required for access to the first site).

North West Film Archive, Minshull House, 47 Chorlton St, Manchester, M1 3FY – has early moving film of sport and a good search engine, mainly late material.

Warrington Library, Museum Street, Cultural Quarter, Warrington, WA1 1JB – an example of a local library with sporting material.

www.bfi.org.uk/nationalarchive/about – a site to explore if interested in moving images. This also gives access to various regional sites where film is stored and can be viewed (see 'Accessing the Collections' and media-theques within this site).

www.thefostersofmalvern.co.uk/family.htm – is the site dedicated to the Worcestershire Foster family, featured in the Case Studies chapter. This is also an excellent example of what can be done with a family website.

www.hungerfordvirtualmuseum.co.uk – the town of Hungerford has no physical museum but a virtual one, which covers one of the great bare-knuckle fights of the nineteenth century. Virtual museums are worth looking out for.

www.londonancestor.com/newspaper/1882/0805/sport.htm – provides a good example of Victorian sports coverage in a newspaper.

www.mediastorehouse.com/prints-4313/sport-gallery.html – another commercial site which often features prints and pictorial sporting memorabilia.

www.nationalarchives.gov.uk/a2a – 'Access to Archives' run by The National Archives is invaluable in terms of discovering where historical sporting material is being kept. It has a search engine that is easy to use.

www.philipsharpegallery.com/browse.php?rid=13 – although a sales site this often has good examples of sporting prints. Subjects in 2011 included billiards, boxing, cricket, horse racing, fencing and jockeys.

www.sportsmuseums.co.uk – worth visiting if a specific sport museum is not mentioned below.

www.victorianperiodicals.com/series2/default.asp – subscription site useful for finding about sporting magazines and periodicals.

Sports (in alphabetical order)

Archery

Balfour Paul, Sir James, *The History of the Royal Company of Archers: The Queen's Body-Guard for Scotland* (Edinburgh, 1875).

Balfour Paul, J. Lyon King of Arms; Duke of Bedford (ed.), 'Scottish Archery' (Chapter XIII), *The Badminton Library of Sports and Pastimes* (London and Boston, 1894).

www.archersofteme.org.uk/history – covers the history of one of the oldest sporting clubs to have women members.

Archery GB, Lilleshall National Sports Centre, Newport, Shropshire, TF10 9AT – governing Body for the sport of archery in Great Britain and Northern Ireland (www.archerygb.org/ArcheryGB).

Dick Galloway Archery Museum, Scottish Archery Centre, Unit 15, Fenton Barns Retail Village, North Berwick, East Lothian, EH39 5BW – an interesting and proactive museum dealing with many aspects of competitive archery (www.scottisharcherycentre.co.uk/museum.htm).

Association Football

Barrett, Norman, *Daily Telegraph Football Chronicle* (London, 1993) – a good chronology using primary sources with a little on women's football.

Davies, Hunter, *Postcards form the Edge of Football* (London, 2010).

Harrison, Paul, *The Lads In Blue: The Complete History of Carlisle United FC* (Harefield, Middlesex, 1997) – an excellent example of the kind of club history available.

Hornby, Hugh, *Uppies and Downies: The Extraordinary Football Games of Britain* (English Heritage, 2008) – deals with the history of traditional foot-ball.

Joyce, Michael A., *Football League Players' Records 1888–1939* (Nottingham, 2002) – good for the records of early professionals.

Mason, Tony, *Association Football and English Society, 1863–1915* (Brighton, 1980) – leads to an understanding of soccer's early years.

Newsham, Gail J., *In a League of Their Own!: The Dick, Kerr Ladies Football Club* (Chorley, Lancashire, 1994).

Nannestad, Ian, 'New Goals in Family History', *Family History Monthly*, No. 109 (October 2004).

Rollins, Jack, *Soccer at War*, (London, 1985) – who played for which team and where.

National Football Museum, Sir Tom Finney Way, Deepdale, Preston, PR1 6RU – a relatively new development with many exciting collections still being explored (www.nationalfootballmuseum.com).

Scottish Football Museum, Hampden Park, Glasgow, G42 9BA – the website has a virtual tour of the museum (www.scottishfootballmuseum.org.uk).

Wrexham County Borough Museum, County Buildings, Regent St, Wrexham, Clwyd, LL11 1RB – 'memorabilia connected to football in Wales from local clubs up to the national team' (www.wrexham.gov.uk/assets/pdfs/leisure/football.pdf).

The Arsenal Museum, Emirates Stadium, London, 95 1BU – in the purpose-built stadium, deals with the history of the club from its days at Woolwich.

Liverpool FC Museum, 40 Anfield Road, Liverpool, Merseyside, L4 0TH

Manchester United FC Museum, Matt Busby Way, Old Trafford, Manchester M16 0RA.

Manchester City Football Club Museum, City Of Manchester Stadium, Rowsley Street, Sportcity, Manchester, Greater Manchester, M11 3FF.

West Ham Football Club Official Museum, Boleyn Ground, London, E13 9AZ.

The Football Association, 25 Soho Square, London, W1D 4FA – the longest
running of the UK footballing organisations (www.thefa.com).
For Ireland look up the Irish FA (Northern Ireland) and the Football
Association of Ireland (Irish Republic).
There are many sites relating to the sale of football programmes, acces-
sible via search engines. The site for Programme Monthly and Football
Collectibles (www.pmfc.co.uk/what_are_they.php) gives a good
account of the history of football programmes.

Athletics

George, Walter, *Athletics and Kindred Sports* (London, four vols 1902–06)
– this is a useful account of Victorian athletics by one of the master runners. He wrote another book on his training methods two years later.
Harley, A.A. (compiler), *The Sport of Race Walking* (Race Walking Association,
1962) – full of names with accompanying sketches.
Lovesey, Peter, *Kings of Distance* (1968) – a highly recommended account of
the careers of many distance runners.
Lovesey, Peter, *The Official Centenary History of the Amateur Athletics Association*
(Enfield, 1979).
Lupton, Ken, *Running in the Pools: Centenary History of Burn Road Harriers*
(1895–1995 and Hartlepool, 1995) – an informative club history packed
with detail and featured in the Case Studies chapter.
Magazines such as *Running Magazine* and *Northern Runner* have also
proved useful.
www.prestonharriers.com/1881_the_beginning.htm – an introduction to
both early professional and amateur athletics in the Lancashire town.
www.gbrathletics.com/bc/bc1.htm – describes itself as 'the best historical
British athletics stats site'.
www.sportingworld.co.uk/newyearsprint/briefhistory_20.html – as a
starting point for the history of the Powderhall Sprint.
There have been considerable changes in the structure of British athletics
in the late twentieth century and early twenty-first centuries, with the
following organisations now in control of the sport:
UK Athletics Ltd, Athletics House, Central Boulevard, Blythe Valley Park,
Solihull, West Midlands, B90 8AJ – as the national governing body for
athletics, UK Athletics oversees the development and management of the
much Olympic and Paralympic sport.

England Athletics, Wellington House, Starley Way, Birmingham International Park, Solihull, B37 7HB – England Athletics is now he National Governing Body for the sport, developing and promoting Athletics across the whole of the country.

Scottish Athletics, Caledonia House, South Gyle, Edinburgh, EH12 9DQ – is the governing body for athletics in Scotland, succeeding the Scottish Athletics Federation.

Welsh Athletics Ltd, Cardiff International Sports Stadium, Leckwith Road, Cardiff, CF11 8AZ.

Athletics Northern Ireland, Athletics House, Old Coach Road, Belfast, BT9 5PR.

Athletic Association of Ireland, Unit 19, Northwood Court, Northwood Business Campus, Santry, Dublin 9, Ireland.

Badminton

The national museum and organisational centre for the sport are in the same place: National Badminton Museum, National Badminton Centre, Milton Keynes, MK8 9LA.

www.badmintonengland.co.uk/text.asp?section=41 – has a useful section on early players.

www.badmintonsecrets.com/history-of-badminton.html – a handy site for the history of the sport.

www.dmoz.org/Sports/Badminton/Clubs/United_Kingdom/England – covers the English clubs and their histories.

Basketball

The Basketball League Ltd, Unit 29, Leicester Business Centre, 111 Ross Walk, Leicester, LE4 5HH.

www.bbl.org.uk – a relatively young organisation but a starting point for the sport in Britain today.

en.wikipedia.org/wiki/Basketball_in_England – for a reliable brief history of the sport in the England.

Billiards

www.eaba.co.uk – the site of the English Amateur Billiards Association has some excellent historical material dealing with the careers of many of the early championship players.

www.normanclare.co.uk/museum.htm – a site which deals with the history of both of the cue-based sports.

Boat Racing or Aquatics

Cleaver, Hylton, *A History of Rowing* (London, 1957) – much information on amateur and professional rowers with illustrations and informative appendix.

Dod, Christopher, *The Story of World Rowing* (London, 1992).

Halladay, Eric, *Rowing in England: A Social History* (Manchester, 1990) – regarded as a good introduction to the subject.

Whitehead, Ian, *The Sporting Tyne: A History of Professional Rowing* (Gateshead, 2002) – deals mainly with north-east England but useful on Thames opponents too.

Whitehead, Ian, *James Renforth of Gateshead: Champion Sculler of the World* (Newcastle, 2004) – also brings in other scullers from outside the region.

The River and Rowing Museum, Mill Meadows, Henley on Thames, RG9 1BF – the museum has a rowing gallery and the website is useful and well organised (www.rrm.co.uk).

www.britishrowing.org – a site for British Rowing, organiser of the sport today. Also directs readers to the other national bodies governing the sport in the UK.

chesterrowingclub.tidywebsites.co.uk – Royal Chester Rowing Club, like many others, has a historical section on its website.

www.nerowing.com – deals with rowing in the north-east of England where the sport was strong among professionals in the nineteenth century.

www.rowinghistory.net – an American site with useful British references.

Bowls

Manson, James, *The Complete Bowler* (London, 1912) – 'a connected sketch of the history of bowls from its inception to "the present day".'

Bowls England, Worthing Office, Lyndhurst Road, Worthing, West Sussex, BN11 2AZ – modern successor to the EBA.

www.bowlsengland.com/index.asp?pageID=265 – has details of champions and runners up from the early twentieth century onwards.

www.booksonbowls.co.uk – a comprehensive list of useful books on bowling and the history of the sport.

www.tradgames.org.uk/games/Bowls.htm – an online guide to the history of different forms of bowls (and curling).

Boxing

Ford, John, *Prizefighting: The Age of Regency Boximania* (Newton Abbott, 1971).

Gee, Tony, *Up to Scratch: Bareknuckle Fighting and the Heroes of the Prize-ring* (Harpenden, 2001).

Leslie, Kim, 'A Fight near Chichester', *Family History Monthly*, No. 108 (November 2004) – deals with a nineteenth-century bare-knuckle fight.

The Illustrated Police Budget, London, 10 June 1893 to 16 April 1910, Nos 1–880; *The Illustrated Sporting Budget and Boxing Record*, 23 April 1910 to 6 August 1912, Nos 881–1001; *Sporting Budget*, 13 August to 19 November 1912, Nos 1002–1016 – much of interest on contemporary fights as well as classic fights from the past.

boxrec.com/media/index.php/Main_Page – an online boxing encyclopaedia.

www.lynnacboxing.co.uk/History.html – London's Lynn ABC still going strong and an interesting website.

www.abae.co.uk/aba/index.cfm/boxers/roll-of-honour/elite-abae-championship/1890-1899/1895.

Cricket

Allen, David Rayvern, *Cricket's Silver Lining 1864–1914: The Fifty Years From The Birth of Wisden to the Beginning of the Great War* (London, 1987) – useful contemporary articles from these important cricketing years.

Allen, David Rayvern, *A Song For Cricket* (London, 1981) – many songs from the early period of cricket, often naming names.

Altham, H.S. and Swanton, E.W., *A History of Cricket* (London, various editions 1926–49) – as complete a history of the early game of cricket as it is possible to find.

Ambrose, Don (compiler), *Liverpool and District Cricketers (1882–1947)* (ASC Publications, 2002) – an example of the type of local/regional sporting research that has been carried out.

Bailey, Philip; Thorn, Philip; Wynne-Thomas, Peter, *Cricketers' Who's Who* (London, 1984) – an enormous work of use to all with first-class cricket connections.

Barlow, R.G, *Forty Seasons of First Class Cricket* (Manchester, 1908/reprint 2002).

Birley, Derek, *The Willow Wand: Some Cricket Myths Explored* (London, 1987) – a fine work dealing with the nature of amateur and professional in cricket.

Birley, Derek, *A Social History of English Cricket* (London, 1999) – as above.

Caffyn, William, *Seventy-One Not Out: the Reminiscences of William Caffyn* (1899/reprint Whitefish, Montana, 2009).

Chesterton, George; Doggert, Hubert, *Oxford and Cambridge Cricket* (London, 1989) – a thorough account of cricket matches between the two university sides from the early nineteenth century onwards.

Golesworthy, Maurice (compiler), *The Encyclopaedia of Cricket* (London, 1964) – one of many useful encyclopaedias on the game.

Howat, Gerald, *Village Cricket* (Newton Abbot, 1980) – a complete history of village cricket from the eighteenth century onwards.

Kynaston, David, *W.G.'s Birthday Party* (London, 2010) – an up-to-date view on the divide between amateur and professional.

Martineau, G.D., *The Valiant Stumper: A History of Wicket Keeping* (London, 1957) – a good example of a book based on a cricket specialism.

Warsop, Keith and Thorn, Philip, *First-Class on Tour* (ACS, 2005) – useful on cricketers on the very fringes of the first-class game.

Wynne Thomas, Peter, *Sir Julien Cahn's Team 1923–1941* (ACS, 1994).

Castle Cary Cricket Club 1837–1987: A Collection of Memorabilia from the Club

Archives to Celebrate 150 Years of Cricket in Somerset (Castle Cary, 1987) – a good example of a thorough club history from Somerset.

Magazines worth consulting are *Wisden Cricketer*, earlier copies of *Wisden Cricket Monthly* and *The Cricketer*. *Cricket World* magazine often featured articles on cricket at a level lower than first class.

www.wisden.com/default.aspx?id=12 – the official site of *Wisden* and contains details for accessing past copies and reprints.

Lancashire County Cricket Club Museum, Old Trafford, Manchester, Greater Manchester, M16 0PX – covers the history of club and ground from the days of Manchester Cricket Club in the early nineteenth century.

MCC Museum at Lord's, Marylebone Cricket Club, Lord's Cricket Ground, St John's Wood, London, NW8 8QN – the 'home' of cricket and, therefore, a comprehensive collection.

The Cricket Museum, Warwickshire CCC, The County Ground, Edgbaston Road, Edgbaston, Birmingham, B5 7QU – newly refurbished and dealing with over 130 years of cricket.

The work of The Association of Cricket Historians and Statisticians is also worth referencing (acscricket.com) and is the self-defined 'right place' for enquiries about past cricket and cricketers.

Croquet

en.wikipedia.org/wiki/Croquet_Association – contains much in the way of useful historical material.

Curling (see Bowls also)

Kerr, John Rev., *Curling in Canada and the United States: A Record of the Tour of the Scottish Team, 1902–3 and the Games in the Dominion and the Republic* (Edinburgh, 1904).

Kerr, John Rev, *History of Curling* (Edinburgh, 1890).

The Royal Caledonian Curling Club, Cairnie House, Royal Highland Showground, Newbridge, EH28 8NB (www.royalcaledoniancurling-club.org/rccc/index.cfm).

www.englishcurling.org.uk – contact address for English curling is that of the current secretary.

www.electricscotland.com/history/curling – for a copy of Kerr's book on the history of curling.

Cycling

British Cycling, Stuart Street, Manchester M11 4DQ – relatively modern organisation but the website does have a Hall of Fame dealing with historical matters (www.britishcycling.org.uk).

boxscorenews.com/john-player-sons-cycling-set-p215.htm?twindow=Default&smenu=80&mad=No – for examples of cigarette cards relating to the sport.

The National Cycle Collection, The Automobile Palace, Temple Street, Llandrindod Wells, Powys, LD1 5DL, Mid Wales – packed with detail on early cycling and has access to archive information via its website.

www.bidlakememorial.org.uk – interesting information on the early cycle racing pioneer.

www.cyclemuseum.org.uk.

Fencing

De Beaumont, C.L., *Modern British Fencing: A History of the Amateur Fencing Association of Great Britain* in Hutchinson's Library of Sports and Pastimes Series (London, 1950).

British Fencing Head Office, 1 Baron's Gate 33–35 Rothschild Road, London, W4 5HT – more for the modern sport but deals with British fencing and England fencing (www.britishfencing.com).

www.thearma.org – interesting details on works on fencing.

Fives

www.etonfives.co.uk/articles/eccentric.game.html – the Eton Fives Association website has links to other relevant sites.

Golf

Browning, R., *A History of Golf* (London, 1955).

Cousins, G., *Golf in Britain* (London, 1975).

Lowerson, John, 'Scottish Croquet: The English Golf Boom 1880–1914', *History Today* (Vol. 33, issue 5).

British Golf Museum, Bruce Embankment, St Andrews, Fife, KY16 9AB – part of the 'home of British golf' with information sheets on the history and a golf library (www.britishgolfmuseum.co.uk).

Highland Games (and others)

www.visitscotland.com/guide/see-and-do/library/highland-games-history and www.highlandgames.net/historical.html – two useful sites on the history of the Highland Games. The latter points out that many of the relevant books are now out of print.

grasmeresportsandshow.co.uk/History-Page.htm – for professional athletes from the nineteenth century onwards.

Hockey

Howells, M.K., *The Romance of Hockey's History* (Milton Keynes, 1996).

Miroy, Nevill, *The History of Hockey* (Laleham on Thames, 1986).

Hockey Field Magazine.

Horse Racing

Bevan, R.M., *The Roodee: 450 Years of Racing in Chester* (Northwich, 1989) – a good example of a track-related history.

Longrigg, Roger, *The History of Horse Racing* (London, 1972).

'Thormanby', *Kings of the Turf* (London, 1898) – classic history of early horse racing.

National Horseracing Museum, 99 High Street, Newmarket, Suffolk, CB8 8JH – with a well-maintained website containing much of historical interest (www.nhrm.co.uk).

www.georgianindex.net/Sport/Horse/jockeys.html – Georgian-era jockeys, including the Day, Goodison and Edwards families.

www.horseracinghistory.co.uk/hrho/action/viewDocument?id=908.

www.angelpig.net/victorian/steeplechase.html – a good account of the history of steeplechasing.

Hurling and Gaelic Football

GAE, Croke Park, Dublin 3 – the Gaelic Athletic Association (Cumann Lúthchleas Gael), based here since 1908, covering both sports and overseeing their thirty-two county structure (www.gaa.ie).

Ice Skating

National Ice Skating Association (UK) Ltd, Grains Building, High Cross Street, Hockley, Nottingham, NG1 3AX.

www.iceskating.org.uk – the NISA site has an area dedicated to the history of the sport.

familytreemaker.genealogy.com/users/a/v/e/Arthur-John-Aveling-Victoria/FILE/0007page.html – a history of the Aveling family with a biography of James Charles Aveling.

Lacrosse

English Lacrosse, The Belle Vue Centre, Pink Bank Lane, Longsight, Manchester, M12 5GL.

www.englishlacrosse.co.uk – has a useful area 'About the Sport'.

Motor Sport

Brooklands Museum, Brooklands Road, Weybridge, KT13 0QN.

www.brooklandsmuseum.com – has a motoring and motor cycling history page.

Donington Park Museum, Castle Donington, Derby, DE74 2RP – much on Grand Prix racing (www.donington-park.co.uk/pages/motorsport-museum.html).

National Motorcycle Museum, Coventry Road, Bickenhill, Solihull, West Midlands, B92 0EJ.

www.nationalmotorcyclemuseum.co.uk

Polo

Polo clubs playing today and possessing a lengthy history tend to flag these up on their websites:

www.polo.co.uk/polo_history.htm – Ascot

www.hpa-polo.co.uk/about/history_polo.asp – Hurlingham

Roller Skating and Roller Hockey

www.brsf.co.uk – the British Roller Sports Federation (BRSF) is the national governing body for all roller sports in the United Kingdom, for address see current contact.

www.nationalarchives.gov.uk/A2A/records.aspx?cat=124-828&cid=-1#-1 – details of remarkable photographic resource relating to the sport and held at the Manchester Record Office.

Rugby League

Gate, Robert, *Rugby League: An Illustrated History* (London, 1990).

Risman, Gus, *Rugby Renegade* (London, 1958) – a good example of the way autobiographies pick up on early careers.

Rugby Football League, Red Hall, Red Hall Lane, Leeds, LS17 8NB – the Rugby Football League (RFL) is the governing body for Rugby League football in Britain and Ireland, its website has an extensive 'History of the Sport' section (www.therfl.co.uk).

Rugby Union

Dunning, Eric, *Barbarians, Gentlemen and Players: a Sociological Study of the Development of Rugby Football* (Oxford, 1979).

Richards, Huw, *A Game for Hooligans: The History of Rugby Union* (Edinburgh, 2006).

Rugby World – a monthly magazine which often carries historic articles.

Rugby Football Union, Rugby House, Twickenham Stadium, 200 Whitton Road, Twickenham, Middlesex, TW2 7BA.

World Rugby Museum, Twickenham Stadium, South Stand, Whitton Road, London, Middlesex, TW2 7RE – for the World Rugby Museum (which has early moving images).

www.rfu.com and www.rfu.com/microsites/museum.

www.remotegoat.co.uk/venue_view.php?uid=31853&days=300 – an interesting club history, the story of Welsh Rugby Club Ferndale RFC.

Sailing/Yachting

Heaton, Peter, *Yachting: A History* (London, 1955).

RYA House, Ensign Way, Hamble, Hants, SO31 4YA – the Royal Yachting Association is the national body for all forms of boating, including dinghy and yacht racing, motor and sail cruising, RIBs and sports boats, and powerboat racing (www.rya.org.uk/Pages/Home.aspx).

www.bbc.co.uk/scotland/sportscotland/asportingnation/article/0073/print.shtml – a useful site for early Scottish sailing.

Shooting (Rifle and Small Bore)

National Rifle Association, Bisley, Brookwood, Surrey, GU24 0PB www.nra.org.uk.

National Small-bore Rifle Association, Lord Roberts Centre, Bisley Camp, Brookwood, Woking, Surrey, GU24 0NP www.nsra.co.uk.

Show Jumping

British Equestrian Federation, Stoneleigh, Kenilworth, Warwickshire, CV8 2RH .

www.bef.co.uk – the site deals mainly with modern organisation and competition.

Squash and Racquets

www.englandsquashandracketball.com.

www.stepneyrobarts.co.uk/41.htm – David Robarts' family history website with numerous extracts from *The Times* referencing squash matches in the 1920s.

www.talksquash.co.uk – has a couple of sections on the history of the sport.

Swimming

Gordon, Ian and Inglis, Simon, *Great Lengths: the Historic Indoor Swimming Pools of Britain* (English Heritage, 2009) – covers the story of the swimming pools where ancestral swimmers have competed.

Love, Christopher, *A Social History of Swimming in England* (London, 2008).

Sinclair, Archibald; Henry, William, *Swimming* (The Badminton Library of Sports and Pastimes London, 1903).

ASA Headquarters, SportPark, 3 Oakwood Drive, Loughborough, Leicestershire, LE11 3QF.

www.swimming.org/asa – English Amateur Swimming Association.

www.welshasa.co.uk.

www.scottishswimming.com.

www.swimming.org/britishswimming – British Swimming is the national governing body for swimming, diving, synchronised swimming, water polo and open water in Great Britain.

Table Tennis

English Table Tennis Association, Queensbury House, Havelock Road,
    Hastings, East Sussex, TN34 1HF.
www.englishtabletennis.org.uk.

Tennis

Aberdare, Baron Morys George Lyndhurst Bruce, *The Story of Tennis*
    (London, 1959).
Gillmeister, Heiner, *Tennis: a Cultural History* (London, 1997).
Wimbledon Lawn Tennis Museum, All England Lawn Tennis and Croquet
    Club, Church Road, Wimbledon, London, SW19 5AE.
www.wimbledon.org/en_GB/about/museum/index.html – includes a
    downloadable museum brochure.
Royal Tennis Court, Hampton Court (www.royaltenniscourt.com) –
    deals with real/royal tennis, a brief history of the sport and details of an
    active club.

Water Polo

See swimming for the national body.

Weightlifting

British Weightlifting, 110 Cavendish, Leeds Metropolitan University,
    Headingley Campus, Headingley, Leeds, LS6 3QS.
www.britishweightlifting.org – the website has a section dedicated to the
    history of the sport.

Winter Sports

British Ski and Snowboard, 60 Charlotte St, Camden Town, Greater London, W1 T4.

www.teambss.org.uk/about-us – British Ski and Snowboard (BSS) is the national governing body for skiing and snowboarding in the United Kingdom.

Wrestling

Robinson, J. and Gilpin, S., *Wrestling and Wrestlers* (London, 1893).

The British Wrestling Association Limited, 12 Westwood Lane, Chesterfield, S43 1PA.

www.britishwrestling.org – information on past champions from 1904, historical biographies are being set up in a new area of the site.

www.scotwrestle.co.uk – Scottish Wrestling Bond, has an interesting history area.

OTHER

Olympics

Baker, Keith, *The 1908 Olympics: The First London Games* (Cheltenham, 2008).

Llewellyn Smith, Michael, *Olympics in Athens 1896: The Invention of the Modern Olympic Games* (London, 2004).

Polley, Martin, *The British Olympics: Britain's Olympic Heritage 1612–2012* (English Heritage, 2010) – all-embracing and covering the quirky English games which predate the modern Olympics.

Wallechinsky, David, *The Complete Book of the Olympics* (London, 2004).

www.olympic.org – official website of the Olympic movement.

www.sports-reference.com/olympics – invaluable site for the study of Olympic history and past competitors.

RELEVANT PUBLICATIONS BY THE AUTHOR

Books and Booklets

Bluffer's Guide to the Olympics (London, 2008) – an amusing look at Olympic history and referencing one or two Olympic characters.

Corvan: A Victorian Entertainer and His Songs (Oxford, 1983) – also has songs about sport and sporting personalities.

Cumbrian Songs and Ballads (Lancaster, 1980) – includes songs referring to sports and sportsmen.

A Great Day For England: Olympic Cricket (Manchester, 2008) – the little-told story of the only Olympic cricket medallists (Paris, 1900).

One Among Many: the Story of Sunderland RFC (1873 to date) in its Historical Context (London, 2011) – the history of a 'typical' English rugby club set against the background of wider events, social and sporting.

Singing Histories: Sunderland (London, 2009) – contains references to sport on Wearside.

Sunderland Bowling Club: 1889–1989 (Sunderland, 1989) – a brief history of the club that produced successful national winners in the early years of organised bowling.

Tracing Your Northern Ancestors: a Guide to the North-east and Cumbria for the Family Historian (Barnsley, 2007) – includes sport in a chapter on leisure.

A Viking in The Family and Other Family Tales (Stroud, 2011) – little on sport but a great deal of advice on family history research.

Academic Articles

'Sport, Music-Hall Culture and Popular Song in Nineteenth-Century England', *Culture, Sport and Society*, Vol. 2, No. 2 (summer 1999) with Professor Mike Huggins – an argument in favour of using popular song as a source for sporting history.

'Wor Stars That Shine: Northern Songs, Sporting Heroes and Regional Consciousness c. 1800–1880' in *Northern History*, XLIV 2 (2007) with Professor Mike Huggins – the cult of the popular sporting star.

Oxford Dictionary of National Biography – entries on footballers Raich Carter, Len Shackleton and George Hardwick, and professional athlete William 'Jaffray' Cummings.

Popular Articles

'Ashbrooke Internationals', *Hockey Field* (April 1987) – international ladies hockey matches played in north-east England in the 1950s.

'The 1900 Olympics: a Great Cricketing Mystery', *Ancestors* (August 2008) – more on Olympic cricket.

'The Bonny Brave Boat Rowers', *Ancestors* (December 2008) – detailed history of professional Victorian oarsmen.

'Chariots of Fire: the Early Modern Olympics', *Your Family Tree* (July 2004) – charts many British competitors at the first few modern Olympic Games.

'Gamekeepers Do Other Things Too', *The Shooting Gazette* (October 2006) – deals with early gamekeepers roles in various sports.

'Last But Not Least (International Rugby)', *Italy Magazine* (April/May 2004) – Italy enters the Rugby Union fold.

'Pounding Ashbrooke's Green Sward', *Northern Runner* (October/November 1987) – looks at athletics in Sunderland 1887–1987.

INDEX

Royal Iniskilling Fusiliers 62
Royle, Vernon Revd 117

Sadler, Joe 35
Sahler, H.G. 107
Saltburn 40
Sandhurst Academy 15
Sansom, Bruce 98, 102
Scott, Edward 91
Scunthorpe 31
Sefton Harriers 101
Segrave, Henry 54
Sheffield 17, 28, 30–3, 72, 113, 115
Shepherd, Mike 157
Sherman, John 39
Sherwin, Mordecai 39, 118
Shilbottle 132
Shrewsbury 130
Shrubb, Alfred 63
Slough 28
Small, John 38
Smart, William (Turkey) 53
Smith, Raymond E. 101
Smith, Gladys Eastlake 104
Smiths 122
Snaresbrook 84
Snowden, Jem 44
Soher, Rodney 98
Somers Smith, John 101
Sotheran, Thomas 44
Southampton 56, 60, 67
Southport and Ainsdale 120
Spencer, Edward 101
Spring, Tom 46
St Albans 44, 81
St Andrews 41, 78, 142
St Columb Major 51
St Leger 43
St Louis 69, 103
Stanton, Walter 85
Stanyforth, R.T. 134

Starcross 89
Sterry, Charlotte (Cooper) 96
Stockport Harriers 101
Stockton 40, 72
Strachan, E.A. 62
Stratford 95
Sturgess, William 63
Sullivan, John L. 48
Sunderland 8, 68, 111, 116, 130, 141, 145–7
Surbiton 84, 90
Sutcliffe, Willie 88
Sutton Coldfield 56
Swansea 18, 87
Syers, Madge 155–6
Synger, Herbert 50

Taylor, Thomas 38
Taylor, Henry 96–7, 105
Taylor (wrestling) 113
Tebbit, A. 83
Teddington 79
Telford 68
Thackwell, Albertine 104
Thomas, Harry 102
Thomson, Ethel Warneford 64
Titmus, Fred 40
Tiverton 28
Tomkins, Frederick 102
Tomkinson, J.E. (Parker) 92, 161
Townsend, Geoff 70
Toxophilite Society 55
Tredwen family 90
Tregurtha, Nicholas Jacob 100
Twickenham 34, 120, 142

Ulverston 113

Varley, Harry 88
Victoria, Queen 12, 14, 17, 19, 22, 31
34, 44, 48–9, 76, 92, 111
Vidal, R.W.S. 59

Other titles published by The History Press

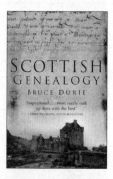

Scottish Genealogy
BRUCE DURIE   £13.49

Scottish Genealogy is the comprehensive guide to tracing your family history in Scotland. The work is based on established genealogical practice and is designed to exploit the rich resources that Scotland has to offer. After all, this country has possibly the most complete and best-kept set of records and other documents in the world. Addressing the questions of DNA, palaeography and the vexed issues of clans, families and tartans.

978-0-7509-4569-1

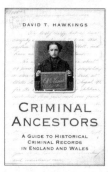

A Viking in the Family & Other Family Tree Tales
KEITH GREGSON   £9.99

Genealogist Keith Gregson takes the reader on a whistle-stop tour of quirky family stories and strange ancestors rooted out by amateur and professional family historians. Each lively entry tells the story behind the discovery and then offers a brief insight into how the researcher found and then followed up their leads, revealing a range of chance encounters and the detective qualities required of a family historian.

978-0-7524-5772-7

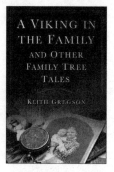

Criminal Ancestors
DAVID T. HAWKINGS   £18.00

When one discovers a criminal in the family tree, you need to know how to trace that person. Using county and borough record offices, the public record office, police archives and numerous example cases, this unique and richly illustrated book provides the essential research and reference tool which no genealogist, social historian, criminologist or the merely curious should be without.

978-0-7509-5057-2

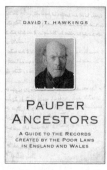

Pauper Ancestors: a Guide to the Records Created by the Poor Laws in England & Wales
DAVID T. HAWKINGS   £27.00

In 1834 the Poor Law Commission split England and Wales into Unions of parishes, each with its own workhouse. Being part of the government bureaucracy, detailed records were kept of everything: inmates, staff, help given. *Pauper Ancestors* explains how these records can reveal your ancestry, providing a must-have resource for genealogists who want to use this comprehensive repository of information.

978-0-7524-5665-2

Visit our website and discover thousands of other History Press books.

www.thehistorypress.co.uk